MANAGING THE PMO LIFECYCLE

A Step-by-Step Guide to PMO Set-up,
Build-out, and Sustainability

WAFFA KARKUKLY

Order this book online at www.trafford.com
or email orders@trafford.com

Most Trafford titles are also available at major online book retailers.

© Copyright 2012 Waffa Karkukly.
All rights reserved. No part of this publication may be reproduced, stored in a retrieval system, or transmitted, in any form or by any means, electronic, mechanical, photocopying, recording, or otherwise, without the written prior permission of the author.

Printed in the United States of America.

ISBN: 978-1-4669-6848-6 (sc)
ISBN: 978-1-4669-6850-9 (hc)
ISBN: 978-1-4669-6849-3 (e)

Library of Congress Control Number: 2012921711

Trafford rev. 11/15/2012

 www.trafford.com

North America & international
toll-free: 1 888 232 4444 (USA & Canada)
phone: 250 383 6864 ♦ fax: 812 355 4082

CONTENTS

DEDICATION ix

ACKNOWLEDGEMENT xi

PREFACE xiii

KEY TERMS xiv

ABOUT WAFFA KARKUKLY, PH.D xv

INTRODUCTION xvii
    Background xviii
    Chapter Structure xxiii
    Chapter Summary xxiv

CHAPTER 1 1
The PMO Lifecycle 1
    Understand the "P" in the PMO 9
    Identify the right level of PMO Authority 12
    Identify the right PMO scalability model 20
    Global PMO vs. Enterprise PMO 27
    Other Functions 28
    Overall PMO tips 31
    Scalability 32
    Chapter Summary 32

CHAPTER 2 33
PMO SET-UP 33
    Newly created PMO 34
    Existing PMO 42
    Chapter Summary 46

CHAPTER 3 47
PMO BUILD-OUT 47
- Newly created PMO 48
- Existing PMO 55
  - Chapter Summary 61

CHAPTER 4 63
PMO SUSTAINABILITY 63
- Sustainability Principles 63
- Human Resources value 65
- Customer value 67
- Risk Management Factor 69
- PMO Sustainability 71
  - Newly created PMO 72
  - Existing PMO 78
- Sustainability toolkit 83
- Chapter Summary 88

CHAPTER 5 89
PMO Survey Results 89
- Analysis of Categorical Data 92
- Descriptive Analysis of Continuous Data 94
- Chapter Summary 111

CHAPTER 6 113
PMO CONTROVERSIAL TRENDS 113
- PMO or Project Management 113
- Temporary or Permanent 115
- Insource or Outsource 118
- PPM or PMO 120
- Chapter Summary 123

CHAPTER 7 125
PMO Case Studies 125
- Case Study Introduction 125
- General Analysis 126

Specific Case Studies Analysis 128
The Case Organizations 130
    Aviva Canada 130
    INVEST&WEALTH 136
    Interac 141
    McDonald's—Canada 149
    G&E—Game & Entertainment 154
Chapter Summary 160

REFERENCES 161

INDEX 165

APPENDIX A—Interaction Model 169

APPENDIX B—Roadmap 171

APPENDIX C—Web-Based Survey letter 173

APPENDIX D—Web Survey Questions 175

APPENDIX E—Case Studies Interview Questionnaire 183

APPENDIX F—List of All Tables 187

DEDICATION

To the Almighty, who guards over me and illuminate the possibilities throughout the journey of my life.

ACKNOWLEDGEMENT

Gratitude to my mom and sister, who have helped me, accomplish my dreams through caring, encouraging, and the unconditional loving. Further thanks to my esteemed friends and colleagues for their encouragement, motivation, and support. Additional thanks to all those volunteers who have taken part in my survey. Special, recognition goes to all those PMO leaders who took the time to participate in the case studies and to their organizations who have shared with me their PMO journey. Last but not least thanks to those academics and professional experts who have endorsed my work.

To all my friends and esteemed colleagues: Sincere gratitude and Thanks.

PREFACE

I recently ran a survey on the Project Management Office Lifecycle —PMOLC and the role of PMO, executives, and organizations who want to achieve success from the PMO function. The findings are shared in one of the later chapters in this book. The survey highlights the rise of PMOs in organization, the complexity model of PMOLC, and the skills required to lead a PMO

Those who follow the PMO news and the evolution / revolution that PMOs are going through will attest that PMO's are on the rise, not decline. There are academic and practical studies that show the vulnerability of some PMO's and the transformation they go through. Some are being shutdown, others being rebuilt, or transformed as a new virtualized concept has emerged and is on the rise. The function is undergoing transformation as a result both of external factors such as (economy, competition, market demand) and of internal factors such as (organization restructure, budget, time to market).

This book is a small contribution to years of collective effort to highlight what goes into the set-up, build-out, and sustainability of PMOs, the drivers, the benefits, and the know-how. The book's main purpose is to serve as a guide for all those wishing to know more about PMO build and support. Whether you are an executive in an organization looking to build a new PMO or revitalize an existing one. If you are a recently appointed PMO head and in charge of building a PMO, or are a functional (Business unit) head who is asked to work with a PMO in your organization and want to understand how to interact with this function this book will help you and your organization maximize the benefits of your interactions. If you are a student looking to become part of PMO organization and wanting to know the roles, responsibilities and how this function works with other functions, then this is a must read for you. The book includes templates that provide guidance to help assess, implement, and manage a PMO.

KEY TERMS

CoE—Center of Excellence
CoP—Community of Practice
JIT—Just in time
PMBOK—Project Management Body of Knowledge
PMO—Project/Program/Portfolio Management Office
PMOLC—Project Management Office life cycle
PMLC—Project Management life cycle
PM—Project Manager
PMI—Project Management Institute
PRINCE2—Project In Complete
QRM—Quality Risk Management
RACI—Responsible.Accountable.Consulted.Informed
SLA—Service Level Agreement

ABOUT WAFFA KARKUKLY, PH.D

Dr. Waffa Karkukly is the Principal and Managing Director of Global PMO Solutions, www.globalpmosolution.com. With over 20 years' experience in IT, project management, and PMO establishments, Waffa has extensive experience in project management, particular expertise specializing in establishing practical PMOs and revitalizing and assessing value propositions of existing PMOs. Waffa has helped fortune 100, midsize, and small sized organizations improve their project management practices and PMO establishments through building scalable standards and proven solutions that improved their delivery process.

Prior to establishing Global PMO Solutions, Dr. Karkukly held many positions ranging from big 5 to small startups where she held the responsibility of establishing PMOs that included Portfolio, building governance models and benchmark process improvement.

Waffa holds a BSC in Information Systems from DePaul University, an MIT from Northwestern University, and a PhD from SKEMA School of Business. Waffa's dissertation was in the PMO realm an area of her expertise and passion. She is a certified project management professional (PMP), and dedicated to improving the understanding and standards of project management practices especially in the Value proposition of building and sustaining.

Waffa is an active PMI member and holds the positions of Director of Communication for the PMO CoP and Regional communication coordinator for the PMOLIG. She contributes to many publications with project management articles and is a frequent speaker in project management chapters and forums.

INTRODUCTION

This book is a contribution of years of collective effort to highlight what goes into the set-up, build-out, and sustainability of Project Management Offices (PMOs). In addition, it provides the drivers, the benefits, and the know-how. The book's main purpose is to be a reference guide for all those investing in setting up, building-out, or supporting PMO's. The book addresses various audiences on a corporate ladder or also for student seekers of knowledge in the practical domain of PMO's.

Whether you are:

- an executive in an organization looking to build your new PMO or revitalize an existing one;
- a new PMO head and in charge to build a PMO;
- or you are a functional (Business unit) head who is asked to work with a PMO in your organization and want to understand how to interact with this function the book will help you and your organization maximize the benefits of your interactions.

If you are:

- a project manager looking to understand what it means to be reporting into the PMO, the book will help you understand your career option with a PMO;

- if you are a student looking to become part of PMO organization and wanting to know roles, responsibilities and how this function works with other functions, then this is a must read for you.

Background

The majority of the PMO research thus far has focused on investigating issues such as: the PMO, the understanding of the PMO and its various functions, structure, types, roles, the multi structure of a PMO and the PMO's performance (Aubry and Hobbs, 2007; Crawford, 2002; Karkukly, 2010). As PMO evolve and the expectations increase in line with the demand on organizations to do better with less, so the need to understand how PMO lifecycle works increases too; because in understanding the PMO lifecycle, organization are able to maximize efficiencies from PMO's created.

The concept of a PMO originated in the 1950s when its role was mainly in the military or in critical projects that was staffed with specialized project staff to ensure completion. Their purpose was to control specific projects and be closer to the customer (Kerzner, 2004).

The journey since 1960 has changed the PMO in terms of operation and both user and management expectations. While project based industries (IT, construction and defense), profited from projects they had a level of project maturity and were the first to establish project offices to monitor their project progress. Non-project based industries were measured by their functional product line; hence, project management maturity was slower and adoption of the project office was slower too (Rad and Levin, 2002).

Although a majority of organizations are adopting project management to solve problems; those that are project driven should adopt a broader application of project management disciplines and new models to make themselves more effective (Gareis, 2005.

Although there is more or less agreement as to what the three letter acronym (PMO) stands for, there are variations in defining the PMO function and role that depend on the structure and functions that an organization plans to achieve. These include:

> *An Organizational body or entity assigned various responsibilities related to the centralized and coordinated management of those projects under its domain. The responsibilities of the PMO can range from providing project management support functions to actually being responsible for the direct management of a project* (PMI 2004, p.369).

> *A project management office (PMO) is an organizational body or entity assigned various responsibilities related to the centralized and coordinated management of those projects under its domain. The responsibilities of a PMO can range from providing project management support functions to actually being responsible for the direct management of a project* (PMI, 2008, P. 11).

> *PMO is a centralized unit within an organization or department that oversees and improves the management of projects* (Grey and Larson, 2006, p.561).

The author's definition is:

> **PMO is a critical organizational entity that adopts a variety of roles and structures (see Figure I1) but should be focused on adding value to an organization and its customers to achieve the desired organizational performance.**

Performance

Other authors have offered various perspectives on the exact nature of the function

Kerzner (2005) describes the project management office as the guardian of the project management intellectual property. Other organizations established PMO's initially to cut costs, but then they have evolved into organization to 1—manage single large project, 2—provides guidance, methodologies, tools and techniques, and 3—(most recently) become centers of excellence which manages groups of projects (Kerzner, 2004).

Bates (1998) believes that PMO establishes project management methods, defines and implements processes and procedures, provides project structure, and deploys supporting systems and tools, and provides project manager development, training.

Rad (2000) describes PMO as a function that include formalization and consistency in selecting projects, more effective coordination of multiple projects, improvement in project performance in terms of the triple constraints (cost, schedule, and scope); therefore, improve organization profitability.

Santosus (2003) describes PMO as a function that may enable consistency of approach across projects. As organizations seek more efficiencies and increased performance from projects, they turned to establishing project management offices (PMO) to instill the needed discipline of PM. In some cases, early PMO's were created to focus on one major project such as Y2K (Crawford, 2002).

The PMO is becoming an important vehicle within organizations to provide project management services that support the organization's projects delivery and contribute to their performance through standardized processes and practices. The functions and services of PMOs vary depending on the organizations' strategic objectives. In some organizations, PMOs are viewed as the central point for PM implementation throughout the business in others they have a more peripheral, support role to enable PM tools and techniques to be used more effectively. Some PMOs are separate entities reporting into higher up in the organization while others are embedded within divisions or another function within the organization. Example of current PMO's reporting into the CFO or CIO of a company, while others report into Diretor of IT, or business function.

PMOs existed initially as a means of collecting and distributing project management practices and project knowledge throughout the organization. While the success rate of Y2K transitions created the initial opportunity, many organizations continued with PMOs and extended their mandate and increased their activities to include analysis, communication, and decision support (Desouza and Evaristo, 2006). Alongside the PMO there is also another structure that is gaining popularity and offers a strategy to support both project managers and the host organization; the Center of Excellence (CoE).

Some PMO's are called Center of Excellence (CoE) in organizations, and these PMO's are being called CoE have specific elements that needs to be satisfied. For an effective CoE, Bolles (2002) identifies four necessary key elements: an effective CoE provides Authorization; it assists the organization to align its resources with its strategic objectives. In addition it also *identifies, categorizes* and *prioritizes* projects. In addition the PMO provides a means to manage projects and assists an organization to advance in its project management maturity and it does this through:

- **Standards:** establishes standard tools, templates and methodologies to be applied to all projects within an organization.
- **Education:** provides training and education to all concerned with respect to project management within an organization. This is a key component of the cultural change that is often required to implement the authority and standards of a methodology.
- **Readiness:** establishes a project's readiness to proceed through the required methodologies and may include an evaluative aspect or pre-project assessment as to the likelihood of success for a project. This could involve a pre-project assessment of critical success factors or a preliminary risk analysis.

Perhaps the most important PMO benefit is the link it can provides between corporate governance—connecting global strategy and goals and the project management/ individual project success and results—through an effective portfolio management process. In this form, a PMO is all about results and about securing project management—as a realistic bridge between strategy and success (eSilvia, and Soares, 2008, p.7).

Chapter Structure

This book is organized into seven chapters as follows:

The introduction to the book includes background and the breakdown of the chapters. This provides a roadmap to the structure.

Chapter One explains the various PMO types, the various models available as well as offering the reader a PMOLC model (Project Management Office Life Cycle). PMOLC consists of the three PMO phases: set-up, build-out, and sustainability. The subsequent three chapters unfold each phase of the PMOLC. Each explains the processes associated with a newly established PMO as well as those associated with the repurposing or repositioning of an existing function.

Chapter Two steps through the PMOLC "set-up" phase. The set-up includes a seven step process required to set-up a PMO. It illustrates what is involved internally and externally (in those cases where the organization may be outsourcing the set-up).

Chapter Three steps through the PMOLC "build-out" phase. The build-out includes the steps required to build-out a PMO. The chapter takes into consideration executing to the roadmap established in the set-up phase, differentiates between and Enterprise and Global PMO.

Chapter Four steps through the PMOLC "sustainability" phase. The chapter includes sustainability definitions, sustainability elements, and the steps required to sustain an established PMO

Chapter Five analyzes the results of a global web-based survey and provides statistical findings to illustrate key issues during the PMO set-up, build-out, and sustainability. It further analyzes these findings to provide lessons for those seeking PMO establishment

Chapter Six takes on some emerging topics such as virtual PMO's, PPM practices and outsourcing. These practices will be further reflected on in chapter seven

Chapter Seven presents case studies from well-known organizations that shed light on existing and emerging practices.

↳ lançar luz sobre

Chapter Summary

In this chapter we have presented the aim and objectives of the book. This chapter also introduces the format and organization of the book providing a summary for every chapter to allow the reader to follow the flow as well as refer to the sections needed. The book can be read sequentially or dipped into as a reference.

CHAPTER 1

The PMO Lifecycle

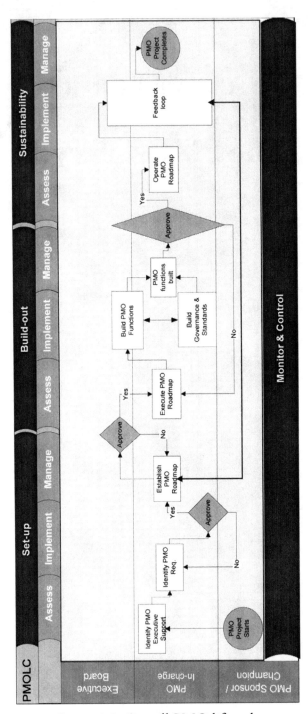

Figure 1.1: Overall PMO lifecycle

This chapter will explain the various PMO types, the models available, and their functions. It introduces the reader to the PMO Lifecycle and its phases: PMO set-up, PMO build-out, and PMO sustainability. Figure 1.1 above describe the three phases at high level illustrating the main activities required to set-up, build-out, and sustain PMOs. In the subsequent chapters, the complete PMO lifecycle will unfold and every step in each phase of PMO set-up, PMO build-out, and PMO sustainability will be explained in details. All three major phases in the PMOLC have their description and can be seen in Figure 1.2.

PMO Set-up

Otherwise known as the assessment phase, or the discovery phase; the purpose of this phase is to define the organization's objective in creating a PMO; identifying the goals and determining the short term and long term plan in the form of a defined roadmap.

PMO Build-out

This phase may be referred to as the deployment or implementation phase of PMO and it involves establishing an execution plan for implementing the approved roadmap activities which include building the required functions leading to PMO rollout

PMO Sustainability

This phase may be referred to as continuous improvement which describes the on-going support of the PMO functions to sustain the performance of the PMO and contribute to the success of the PMO in the organization.

Figure 1.2: Summary of the PMOLC Phase description

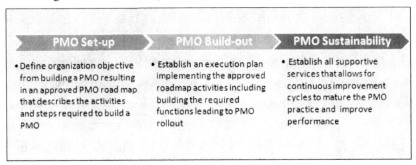

While the first two phases can be grouped and can be treated as a projectized in nature (in other words, the set-up and build-out of PMO can be treated as a project with delivery PMO roadmap, execution plan, proposed functions, etc. The sustainability phase may be seen as the operationalization of the PMO; (in other words, running the day-to-day activities) and addressing the continuous improvement.

In every phase, whether set-up, build-out, and sustainability an iterative three step process will ensure continuous flow between assessment, implementation, and support.

There are a number of major stages within the PMOLC

Identify PMO requirements
Work with the executive team and senior management of the organization to establish the short term and long term goals. What is the vision of the PMO, what is the budget, and what are the parameters for success?

Establish the PMO roadmap
Based on the requirements gathered from executives and senior managers and the objectives required from the PMO, agree a roadmap document which should detail how the PMO will be established; the cost, resources, and finally timeframe for the build-out.

Execute the PMO roadmap
As per the roadmap, establish the functions described in the road map. The PMO may have as many or few functions as it needs depending on the organizations direction and its constraints. The build out is an execution of the approved roadmap.

Operate the PMO roadmap
It is during this phase that the PMO establishes all the supporting services that allow for development and continuous improvement and the feedback loop that incorporate organization voice into these improvements

Prior to unfolding the details of each phase, the author provide information pertaining to PMO types, roles, and differentiate the PMO's based on their authority and structure and provides the various functions PMOs have been tasked to do.

PMO Types and Roles

Literature suggests that not all PMOs are created equal in terms of their types and the functions performed. The terms in some organizations are used interchangeably to refer to activities that a PMO performs. Some organizations only focus their PMO on basic PMO-type functions, while others are more mature with more advanced project and portfolio functions (Crawford, 2004).

The basic type functions include: project methodology, project reporting, project tools, and project training. While advanced project and portfolio functions include: Portfolio analysis and priority, benefit realization, and quality risk management.

The PMO often has a dual role of ensuring compliance in relation to using the methodology, tools and templates and also supports individual business units. The PMO often monitors project progress and reports on this progress and accompanying risks to the organization's senior managers. Another form of PMO finds the office actually managing projects on behalf of the organization and forming project teams. In this structure the PMO typically manages a project from Initiation to Closeout and is responsible for achieving successful project outcomes (Kerzner, 2004).

Letavec (2006) suggests that PMOs may work in any of the following roles:

> 1. Consulting Role—advisor to project/ program teams on how to manage their projects and programs through tools and methodology; 2. Knowledge Management Role—Capturer of project related information, and manage the dissemination of these information; 3. Compliance Role—Set process, tools, and reporting standards (Letavec, 2006).

While Light and Berg (2000) suggest that PMOs may have other roles:

> 1—The PMO as a repository—custodian of the project methodology and is not involved in the decision making process; 2—The PMO as a coach—providing guidance on projects, performing project reviews on request, establishing and supporting project planning, monitoring and reporting on projects but does not order corrective action; and 3—The PMO as manager—operating as an agent of senior management, managing the project portfolio, managing the master resource plan, reviewing project proposals and is accountable for the portfolio (Light and Berg, 2000).

Kerzner (2004) describes project offices as three types/ levels.

> 1—Functional PO, this is typically at the departmental level addressing functional area needs, such as IS. 2—Customer Group PO, this is typically to handle customer management and can act as a company within a company. 3—Corporate PO, this typically services the entire organization and focuses on corporate strategic alignment (Kerzner 2004, p. 278).

Successful PMOs take on responsibility for different project-related functions and core tasks related to development of shared methodology and processes for handling of projects, training and competence development within project management, proposing of new projects, and quality assurance of projects. The success of a PMO is related to ensuring the necessary authority of the PMO: real organizational authority as well as academic and social credibility, top management support, and that the PMO covers true needs in the organization (Anderson et al., 2007, P1).

Recent research and studies classify PMO's into a two types: single project organization and multi project organization. Within each there are different set-ups ranging from a project office centralized around a project to a center of excellence. The table below (Table 1.1) illustrates the type of functions performed and expectations based on the type of PMO. Each author has defined the type of PMOs and different functions from the perspective of an organization's needs.

Table 1.1: Types of PMO and their role definitions

Author	PMO Type	Function / Role
Hill (2004)	PO	Applies effective practices for project performance and oversight; and employs standard life cycle processes when available
	Basic PMO	Introduces critical processes and practices of project management
	Standard PMO	Establishes and monitors use of a complete project management methodology
	Advanced PMO	Enhances content and monitors use of a comprehensive methodology
	Center Of Excellence (CoE)	Analyzes project management methodology and examines process variation in business units
Rad & Levin (2002)	Project or Program	A PMO supporting a single project or a group of related projects is recommended
	Division PMO	This PMO will establish standards and methodologies to follow in project management, will review and audit projects that are under way, and will provide mentoring support to project professionals.
	Enterprise PMO	This PMO is concerned with the enterprise of selection, prioritizing, and monitoring the value from project portfolio of an organization.
Crawford (2002)	Level 1- PCO	This is an office that typically handles large, complex single projects (such as Y2K project). It's specifically focused on one project, but that one project is so large and so complex that it requires multiple schedules, which may need to integrate into an overall program schedule.
	Level 2- Business Unit PO	The value of level 2 PO is that it begins to integrate resources at an organizational level. And it's at the organizational level that resource control begins to play a much higher value role in the payback of a project management system.
	Level 3 - Strategic PO	Only a corporate level organization can provide the coordination and broad perspective needed to select, prioritize, and monitor projects and programs that contribute to attainment of corporate strategy and this organization is the strategic project office.
Kendall & Rollins (2003)	Repository	The PMO serves as a source of information on projects, methodology and standards in this model. This model occurs most often in organizations that empower distributed, business-centric project ownership or with weak central governance
	Coach	The Coach Model is an extension of the Repository Model. It assumes a willingness to share some project management practices across functions and uses the PMO to coordinate the communication.
	Enterprise	This model usually implies a much larger investment and, therefore, usually has a stronger mission, charter and support than the previous two models. The most consolidated version of this organizational model concentrates senior project management expertise and execution within the PMO. Some or all project managers are staffed within the shared service model and consigned to projects as needed. The model assumes a governance process that involves the PMO in most projects, regardless of size.
	Deliver now	In this model, the emphasis is on delivering measurable value to the executive team within each 6-month period. At initial startup of this PMO, the resources focus on accelerated project deliveries across all major projects. This model has sponsorship at a very high executive level (CEO or Senior Vice President). Its metrics are tied directly to senior management performance

Understand the "P" in the PMO

As a starting point, it is helpful to establish what type of PMO your organization requires, whether it is a Project, Program, or Portfolio Management Office.

Project-based PMO
The focus of a project-based PMO is on project level deliverables; how to initiate, plan, execute, monitor and control, and close-out a project. The attention is on the project details pertaining to the specific project milestones and deliverables. The areas of focus include:

- Building the project management methodology
- Promoting standard project management templates and tools
- Ensuring standardization in project delivery
- Improving project delivery and performance
- Allocating and assigning project resources
- Planning project budget as well as tracking variances
- Monitoring project risks and issues
- Project status reporting, dashboard, and KPI

Project-based PMOs can be local, or national, IT-or business-based. In some organizations IT reports into a business unit, for example in some industries every business unit has its IT function while in other organizations IT is considered a business unit such as Finance, or Marketing would be. In large organizations, many Project-based PMOs can be found embedded in departments responsible for direct delivery of projects. Some organizations that have multi PMO's, will have an overarching PMO with a specific governance role to ensure that the overall corporate standardization, communication, performance assessment and measurements are consistent.

Program-based PMO
The focus of program-based PMO's is, as the title suggests, on program level outcomes; how to integrate projects and sequence them, resource management, stakeholders change impact management, and rollup of groups of projects. The attention is on the program deliverables which include business case and program base benefit. The areas of focus include:

- Promoting standard program management methodology
- Ensuring standardization in project delivery across dependent and independent projects
- Performing project benefits as well as looking at program benefit realization
- Budgeting and tracking program level cost/value and ROI
- Addressing resource planning across multi projects with the aim to ensure appropriate allocation
- Monitoring risks and issues at a program level

These PMO's can be local, but more frequently national, or at an enterprise level They are most common in large organizations where various projects either cross geographic locations or company departments and there are strong dependencies between these projects; including ultimately securing delivery as part of a specific program; hence, a PMO may run single or multiple programs.

Portfolio-based PMO
Because of the way some organizations are structured politically some Portfolio based PMO's encompass a project and program delivery component; while others remain as a portfolio function only. These kinds of PMO may have various names if they are a separate function from the PMO (Enterprise Strategy, Corporate Strategy, Strategic Portfolio Office, Corporate Portfolio Office, Portfolio Management Office)

The focus of these PMO's is on portfolio level outcomes and how to align organization strategic initiatives to realize benefits. The areas of focus include:

- Creating an organization portfolio process
- Promoting standards across PPM selection, monitoring and controlling
- Evaluating and prioritizing all initiatives against strategic key indicators
- Performing demand management
- Aligning an organization's budget requests and approvals along with the PPM initiatives
- Implementing on-going governance models to monitor and control PPM health checks
- Performing benefit realization and monitor KPI's and reporting.
- Monitoring risks and issues at a portfolio level

These PMO's are predominantly at a national, or enterprise level; many of them can be found in large organizations in which each business unit may have a delivery base PMO that oversee the execution of a multi projects or programs While the delivery base PMO involved in carrying out projects, they report into the Portfolio base PMO. This PMO has oversight at the macro level of all initiatives generating from the various business units and their objectives is more of portfolio oversight for selecting and prioritizing projects across the entire organization as well as track the benefit realization.

Figure 1.1 summaries the focus of project based, program based, and portfolio based PMOs

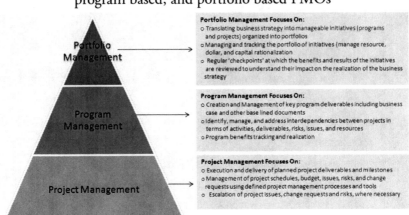

Identify the right level of PMO Authority

If your organization is ready to create a PMO, there are some pre-requisites to ensure you set up the right type of PMO. The assessment can be either through their PMO head, or through a consulting firm hired for this purpose. PMO types and the level of authority need to be vetted before embarking on the creation of the PMO function; for example:

- Consulting /Services—Proposes, advises teams on how to run project
- Knowledge Management—Manages, archives project details and lesson learning
- Compliance—Creates and sets project management standards and monitors and controls adherence to these standards

These levels of authority need to tie in with the PMO types as in table 1.1 (PO, basic PMO, advanced PMO, CoE). While all these authority types can share similar PMO models and create similar functions, the level of authority of a PMO determines its ability to influence change management and project management adoption in an organization.

The author's research indicates that those PMOs given the level of authority required to implement change management and encourage project management adoption within an organization have produced higher results in encouraging project management adoption. In other words, the less empowered the PMO, the less its influence on change management and project management adoption. Table 5.7 in Chapter Five shows results of the correlation of level of authority and project management and change management adoption.

The correlation between levels of authority and different types of PMO functions:

1. Project delivery.

For the consultative and knowledge based type of authority PMO, project delivery is rarely a main functions (See Table 1.2.) While nothing prevents an organization from creating any type of PMO under any level of authority, the fact remains that there is a stronger correlation between some types of PMO and their level of authority as can be seen in chapter 5, table 5.15-5.17. For example, enabling a project delivery function in a consultative or knowledge based PMO without giving the PMO the authority to run or kill projects would not work in the consulting services context.

The success in driving project delivery and building a culture that is accountable to delivery remain depends on how empowered a PMO is to oversee and action projects and enforce rigor that allows sponsor to make decisions in killing projects, continuing with projects. If PMO lacks the authority to take action, then the PMO recommendations will be ignored. Therefore, the best suited type of PMO is an authoritarian PMO to ensure that projects not delivering are auctioned. While project delivery can still be run under PMO of the type consultative or knowledge base; however, the mandate of these types of PMO are not to oversee delivery and delivery oversight in these two types happen to be in the business units in which PMO would lack the authority to make a call over the impact on delivery; hence, PMO is not equipped with the authority to hold owners accountable. PMO is likely to be challenged and there will be tension between the PMO and the business units in terms of accountability; consequently, the PMO's delivery responsibility will be at risk.

2. Project manager development vs. project manager training.

In some organizations, project managers are contracted to or work as consultants for specific projects and they are expected to be up to the standards of the hiring organization; hence, investing in project manager training or project manager development function may not be required. However, in those organization that invest in their people, developing employees skill sets is a feature that is looked upon very positively when project managers are making career moves.

Some organizations may view project manager development and training as synonymous. This is a mistake. Project manager training is a function that is most suited to the consultative and knowledge based PMO authority type because in the consultative role, training is assumed to keep the project managers abreast of standards; the PMO provides training on tools, methods, templates, and the rollout of any updates but is not necessarily responsible for career progression for the project manager. In the case of a compliance based PMO where project managers have a solid reporting line into the PMO, the PMO is accountable for defining the project manager career path (i.e. project manager development).

In some organizations there is a function within the PMO, Project Manager Development, which is responsible for training, providing a career path, and bridging any skill gaps for all project staff and this can only happen when PMO has the authority and the funding to spend and provide on the job or advanced certificates to evolve the develop the skills of its project managers. When PMO has the authority and the required funding, to develop programs tailored to project managers' career paths, the level of authority of PMO does correlate of how much it has influence over the education, mentoring, and guidance of project management within an organization.

3. Project repository.

All PMOs, regardless of type, need to maintain project data for reporting and auditing purposes. While the project repository function is a core function of the knowledge management type PMO or the compliance type PMO, it is not a core function of the consultative PMO. Knowledge type PMOs are accountable for storing all sorts of project artifacts such as project schedule data, cost data, resource allocation, methods, KPI's, lessons learned for the purpose of providing organization with data that turns into knowledge to assess and bench mark project performance. Compliance type PMOs are accountable to delivery of projects; hence, understanding past performance, current project performance allows prediction of future performance leveraging data from lessons learned to improve project delivery time, quality, and expectations in an organization. While consultative PMO is accountable for providing project management standards, methodology, templates for other departments to use, it is important that this type of PMO is expected to maintain some data on which decision makers will base their decisions.

In the compliance type of, PMO, the PMO can influence lessons learned, action taken, project audit and evaluation, while in the knowledge and consultative type this may be difficult since the PMO is not fundamentally responsible for project delivery, nor is it required to maintain the level of knowledge such as lessons learned, KPI's, project performance, etc. In these cases, the business unit or the department responsible for delivery will maintain project data.

4. Project Portfolio

Portfolio function may exist within consultative PMO, but it is best suited in the authoritative type PMO. Authoritative types PMO assumes ownership for organization projects selection criteria, priority, and resources. It has the ability to audit practices based on suggested benefit assurance which no other type of PMO can perform due to the role these types of PMO play which has no PPM oversight.

Table 1.2 shows a summary of PMO authority, type and functions

Common functions to all levels of PMO authority:

1. Project methodology.
All PMO's are required to build methodology or methodologies based on some industry standards. A common methodology is important since it provides a consistent method for performing the project work. This, in turn, enables you to, measure and benchmark success and failure effectively and on an objective and shared basis. In North America PMI PMBOK is the most common methodology. In the UK and Europe PRINCE2 provides the most common standard. Both methodologies have spread beyond their original countries of origin to be used on projects around the world. A note worth making that defining one methodology might fit small size organization but may not fit large size that has various delivery standards and the support of multi methodologies becomes crucial for flexibility and long term sustainability. As a result, this translates to a rapid execution of the strategy, where incremental wins (deliverables) are release at least every quarter no matter how large of a transformation program organizations are leading

2. Project reporting.
Project reporting is an essential function that all PMO's share and must undertake from the early stages of PMO implementation. Although there may be differences in the details of what type of information is reported, the frequency of reporting, and how it is reported; all project reporting reflects project progress, and highlights the parameters influencing project success. For example, successful PMO's should implement the some or all of following set of reports

- Standard project status reports that speaks to project accomplishments, schedule, budget, risks, and issues. Prepare action plan if project has derailed.

- Program level report that looks at independent and interdependent projects and impact of these initiative on program success, indicators include budget, scope, and accomplishments, and tracking of program benefits
- Executive dashboard or score card. Kanban is one popular methods and although it existed for some times, organizations are using this real time visualization tool to determine just in time (JIT) progress of projects. Another popular method is Key Progress Indicator (KPI) that companies often publish on their entire project portfolio for the whole company and all performing and underperforming projects are visible and transparent for all teams.
- Organization wide transparency report that goes as part of annual C level accomplishments to all those involved and it is time to reflect on results and lessons learned

Reports frequency should vary between weekly to a monthly and annual and should be transparent and understood by the various levels of the organization. Keeping it simple is the key to success.

3. Project tools.

For some organizations, introducing project management tools is a last step to address in the paradigm of people, process, and then technology. While other organization use technology as enabler to promote collaboration and team work. To allow teams to collaborate in real time, and share their thoughts, recent tools enhance the productivity and measure progress, and these tools are becoming sophisticated to be used on mobile devices, tablets, etc to allow employees the flexibility to when and how to provide project progress, resource update, and share project artifacts. Regardless of how basic or sophisticated tools can be, they all need to be able to provide the PMO and the organization with standard measures on project health check, project progress reporting, resource allocation, cost analysis, etc. Further, a tool is required to provide executives with project dashboard reflecting the entire portfolio, as well as provide project managers an automated and effective ways to report on project progress and elevate the burden of manual effort and provide efficiency and team collaboration to project artifacts. Some of these most used tools today and are not listed in any special order are: Microsoft Project, Clarity, Microsoft Project Server, HP Project and Portfolio Management, Plainview, etc. More details on tools implementations and options organization has in chapter 3. A summary of all PMO types, authority, and functions can be seen below in table 1.2. Common functions across the various authority levels are highlighted.

Table 1.2: Illustration of PMO authority and related types and functions

PMO Authority	PMO Type	PMO Functions
Consulting Services	Project or Program	Project Methodology
	Division PMO	Project Processes
		Project Reporting
	Enterprise PMO	Project Tools
		Project Manager Training
Knowledge Management	Project or Program	Project Methodology
	Division PMO	Project Processes
		Project Reporting
	Enterprise PMO	Project Repository
		Project Tools
Authoritative / Compliance	Project or Program	Project Methodology
	Division PMO	Project Processes
		Project Reporting
		Project Repository
	Enterprise PMO	Project Tools
	CoE PMO	Project Manager Development
		Project Delivery
	Global PMO	Project Portfolio

Identify the right PMO scalability model

It is important to understand the concept of scalability before we discuss PMO scalability models.

Scalability is important in technology and in business; the underlining foundation is the same, the ability for an organization to increase its volume without negatively impacting its bottom line or disturbing its performance. Scalability may include perspectives such as: functional scalability, and geographic scalability. The categories provided are used to guide PMO leaders when determining the sizing of PMO. The model is not meant to be prescriptive; these are guideline that will be explained in details allowing the PMO leaders to use a combination to determine their PMO scalability.

Project management is no different from technology or other business domain. It requires scalability definitions and measures to understand the level of structure and rigor to enable small organizations project management and large organizations project management to succeed; to avoid falling in the pit of your project management processes are overkill or under estimated, then and no one size fits all for organization.

Below tables 1.3, 1.4, and 1.5 show three examples of the scalability criteria and the sizing proposed to determine whether the PMO is large, medium, or small and to help in the assessment and guide the scalability ranking for a PMO within an organization.

Table 1.3 is an example of a project or program based PMO mainly in local or national level. It is also called in other literature basic PMO or standard PMO (Kerzner, 2004). This kind of PMO would serve a small organization of the 100-300 in size, the impact on business processes is low and it is mainly tactical in nature and tends to be local in geography. This kind of PMO may have or may not have project managers reporting directly into it with limited number of projects.

Table 1.3: Example of a Project or Program PMO

PMO	Project or Program Type		
	Small	Medium	Large
Organization Resources	Less than 300		
External Impact	Y/N		
Internal Impact	Y		
Business Process Change	Low		
Strategic Need	Low		
Geography	Local		
Reporting into	BU Lead		
Project Delivery Direct responsibility	Y/N		
Number of Strategic projects	Less than 20		
Number of Project Managers	Less than 10		

Table 1.4 is an example of what is described as advanced PMO (Kerzner, 2004) which is a program, or a portfolio PMO in nature. This kind of PMO is expandable to national and international geographic setting, serves in medium size organizations of roughly 300-1000 employees. The impact on business processes is high with external impact to client. This kind of PMO tends to report into senior executive within the organization and have direct responsibility to delivering projects. Number of project managers would be anywhere from 11-25, and they may or may not have project managers reporting directly into it with limited sizable number of projects falling from 20-100 projects.

Table 1.4: Example of a Program or Portfolio PMO

PMO	Program or Portfolio Type		
	Small	Medium	Large
Organization Resources		300 - 1000	
External Impact		Y	
Internal Impact		Y	
Business Process Change		Medium	
Strategic Need		Medium	
Geography		National	
Reporting into		Executive	
Project Delivery Direct responsibility		Y/N	
Number of Strategic projects		20-100	
Number of Project Managers		11-25	

Table 1.5 is an example of CoE and also known by multiple names such as strategic PMO, or Enterprise PMO. This kind of PMO is large in nature and serves organizations over 1000 at the international or global geographically. The impact on business processes is high with internal impact to bottom line and external impact to client. This kind of PMO tends to report into senior executive or a C-level within the organization and have direct responsibility to delivering projects. Number of project managers would be anywhere above 25, and they may or may not have project managers reporting directly into it with limited sizable number of projects falling from 20-100 projects.

Table 1.5: Example of a CoE PMO

PMO	Center Of Excellence Type		
	Small	Medium	Large
Organization Resources			Over 1000
External Impact			Y
Internal Impact			Y
Business Process Change			High
Strategic Need			High
Geography			Global
Reporting into			C-Level
Project Delivery Direct responsibility			Y/N
Number of Strategic projects			Above 100
Number of Project Managers			Above 25

After the three examples, each of the scalability categories will be defined and explained separately. Note that none of these categories has meaning in isolation; it is the combination of all these categories that determines the PMO scalability model. A PMO identified as small does not mean it stays small; the guided scalability model needs to be revisited as part of PMO sustainability to ensure that expansion of PMO is portable into the next levels. Below is the definition of each of the scalability categories.

Organization Resources
The number of employees within the organization signifies the size of that organization. While number of employee is not the only measure that determines how large or small an organization can be, it is one of the factors certainly. Often in demographic surveys to find out participants come from organization of which size a range is provided. For example, organization with anywhere between 100-300 employees is classified as small, while organization of 300 employees and less than a 1000 is considered medium, finally over a 1000

employee and organization is considered large. The scalability of a PMO is dependent on this category and how many employees will be supported by the PMO.

External Impact
The external impact refers to the impact on the organization's clients and how this affects your relationship with them. In some cases there may be a direct impact, for example in cases where the client contributes directly to the product or service of the project organization; in other cases an indirect impact, because the client is a consumer of the organization's product or services and thus benefits from improvements to it; and in other cases the PMO may have no material relevance to your working relationship. The scalability of a PMO is dependent on this category and whether it will support external clients' initiatives directly by interacting with client's PMO if they have one or working directly with the project teams in collaboration, or indirectly were PMO supports the projects for its organization only and other organizations provide updates.

Internal Impact
The introduction of a PMO may be designed to have a direct impact on the organization's bottom line such as: performance, financials, brand, and reputation; the scalability of a PMO is dependent on this category and whether it will manage internal initiative directly or indirectly. For example, a PMO managing internal initiatives directly, it means that the PMO is employing project managers that report into the PMO and as a result will have an internal impact on the way the projects are run. When projects are managed indirectly, it means projects are managed by the business units as they may have had it before and the PMO may have less of an impact on internal project delivery.

Business Process Change

It is important to assess the impact of having a PMO on the organization's business processes. One of the scalability elements of a PMO is dependent on this category and whether the change in business processes will be minimal such as impacting how business units interact or substantial such as an overhaul to current practices or introducing new business units or consolidating other business units. For example, in small type of PMO, there may be an impact and if it exists it might be minimal impact within a business unit that deployed a PMO ranging large PMO's were the impact is more evident through changing alignment of internal functions; hence, changing interaction model of an organization.

Strategic Need

There is a need to determine if the PMO is required to fulfill strategic directions or specific directions. Strategic PMOs will include oversight of portfolio management, strategic alignment across the various business units, and oversight to resources capacity. Specific PMOs can be built for example around one project, or to oversee and improve project execution. For example in small PMO, the need for strategic oversight is limited and the PMO may have existed to solve delivery issues, while in large PMO that is targeted for program or portfolio level, the strategic reach of the PMO is high and is required to ensure organization wide portfolio selection and prioritization, and alignment across the business units.

Geography

It is important to understand the geographic reach of a PMO and whether it will be local, national, or international. The geographic domain is an element of scalability that includes a cultural complexity dimension that should be accounted for. For example a small PMO will support one department or a local office within a company, while is a national PMO will cross boundaries within one country with oversight to all project work within the various national branches of a company. International or global can only happen is large organizations were PMO becomes the strategic partner that goes across boundaries and certainly influences the scalability of a PMO. There are companies were their PMO started as national and the success was replicated and scaled to a global level.

Reporting line
Every organization needs to determine the PMO's reporting line. PMO can report into a business unit lead, or into a higher up an executive, or at the highest level into a C-level as in some PMOs report into CIO, or CFO, etc. The reporting line reflects PMO's strategic reach and influence. For example, a small PMO embedded in a business unit may have limited authority or impact to the organization, verses a PMO reporting into a Strategic office or a CIO will have completely different authority and influence.

Responsibility for project delivery
It is important to determine the responsibility of the PMO whether a PMO will have direct responsibility for project delivery as in assigning project managers and overseeing the project, or indirect responsibility for project delivery as in process ownership and reporting on project health check.

Number of projects
The number of projects within the organization signifies the size of that PMO. While number of projects is not the only measure that determines how large or small a PMO can be, it is one of the factors certainly. Often in PMO surveys to find out the projects PMO handle so it can be classified as small, medium, large, a range of project numbers is provided. For example, PMO handles anywhere between 1-20 projects is classified as small, while PMO that handle between 20-100 projects are considered medium, finally over a 100 projects, the

PMO is considered large. The scalability of a PMO is dependent on this category and how many projects will be delivered by the PMO.

Number of project managers
The number of projects managers needs to be determined since it ties with the PMO responsibility for direct project delivery. Knowing the number of project managers ranks the PMOs scale of small, medium, or large because PMO has to manage project managers' career and assignments of projects based on skill set.

For example, PMO that oversees anywhere between 1-10 project managers is classified as small, while PMO that handle between 11-25 projects are considered medium, finally over 25 project managers, the PMO is considered large. The scalability of a PMO is dependent on this category and how many projects managers the PMO need to support, train, and assign projects to.

Global PMO vs. Enterprise PMO

Global PMO and Enterprise PMO are two terms that have been used largely interchangeably, While some organizations refer to their PMO as the enterprise PMO, others refer to it as global PMO. The two, however, are not totally synonymous. A global PMO must be at the enterprise level, whilst an enterprise PMO need not necessarily be at the global level. The reason that some organizations describe their PMO as an Enterprise PMO is because it reports directly into the CEO or a C-level executive and may be part of the CEO office in these organizations. In other organizations, the PMO crosses geographical boundaries which imply a PMO that is both global and enterprise-wide. Global PMO determines the geographic outreach, while enterprise PMO determines the level of the PMO relevant to the functions and its position in the organization chart.

Similarities: Global and Enterprise PMOs are both large; which implies cross functionality, often compliance or audit-driven; project managers report into the PMO directly or under a sub function within the PMO may be called "resource management" function or "resource CoE". The resource management function assigns project managers based on project type, size, and project manager skill set, workload, and availability.

Differences: An enterprise PMO can be local within a geographic boundary; it can also exist within one branch of the organization. A large company that has branches may have multi-level enterprise PMOs serving different goals, and management lines, as well as various budgets and portfolios of projects.

Other Functions

A number of other functions may be included or excluded from the PMO depending on the needs of the organization. These are Quality Risk Management (QRM), and Project Portfolio Management (PPM).

PPM Function
Portfolio management is a dynamic process that involves an organization identifying the products and development projects that needs to be executed for the benefit of the business. This includes selection, prioritization, monitoring and changes based on any unforeseen opportunities that may arise. The process encompasses periodic reviews, comparisons of historical projects and requires go/no-go decisions on an on-going basis to allow businesses to achieve their strategy (Cooper et al., 2006).

Benefits of adopting a disciplined approach to Portfolio Management:

- Optimize the realization of benefits through the management of initiatives as an integrated portfolio
- Value individual projects in the program portfolio against the benefits they will yield to the business
- Resolve program conflicts by reference to the business strategy
- Prioritize and allocate resources on the basis of trade-offs between the business priorities
- Monitor all active and proposed projects within a single overall framework

The two important PPM sub-functions are:

- PPM submission and prioritization.
  When project submissions and requests are gathered from various departments in an organization, then these projects are prioritized across the organization using previously defined categories to rank which projects to execute.

- PPM Monitoring and control.
  Once the initial submission and prioritization has taken place, then a process of monitoring and control is required. This part of PPM involves on-going project submission, reprioritization, and benefit tracking takes. PPM change management and financial control is crucial at this stage to identify stage gates to projects, funding of each phase; to stop projects, or reprioritize them within the PPM list of projects, on the basis of changes in strategic direction or economic factors.

QRM Function
The QRM or project audit is a function that assesses the quality of project management deliverables and the processes, templates and

tools used to secure these deliverables. It is an audit function involving the content and the process that guided how the specific deliverable has been chosen or articulated. QRM function often gets involved in the lessons learned or performs quality checks based on the quality standards that are already instituted.

Ideally the Audit function should be independent from the PMO so that there is no conflict of interest in evaluating the PMO work; for smaller organizations without an independent QRM function the role may be performed by an individual who is independent from the delivery function; someone who is not involved in the day to day project.

In summary, a PMO may vary in the number of functions it performs depending on their complexity and maturity. Some of the main functions expected of a PMO are:

- Project delivery,
- Project manager education, training and development,
- Establishment of methodologies, processes, and supporting tools to facilitate training, and development
- Linking strategy with execution through portfolio management.

Some of the benefits are worth repeating and emphasizing:

- Predictability,
- Repeatability,
- Measurability to track project progress and
- Portfolio benefits realization.

Overall PMO tips

Whether you are working with a business driven PMO or IT PMO; whether it is an enterprise-wide, local, or global, there are a number of basic guidelines in the set-up and build-out:

Keep it simple

There is no harm in starting with a grand vision, but keep the execution simple. In a number of cases the PMO set-up and build-out becomes so complex that it is difficult to show immediate or incremental value. If positive results take longer than executives expect, then the PMO will struggle to sustain the build-out. Aiming too high or building too fast may not allow change to be instituted appropriately. Clearly some organization will be able to take on more than others; understanding the culture, environment and success criteria of your organization is key.

Get your priority straight

Start with people and culture, then processes, and finally the tools. A number of PMO consultants sell 'PMO in a box'. Assuming that your PMO can be a 'plug and play' process is a mistake.

The human aspect (in terms of buy-in, education, and skill set at all levels of the organization) is the primary key to a successful PMO set-up and build-out and ensures sustainability. The processes are the second key element to successful build-out; keep them small and look for opportunities to grow and scale up. Tools are important to generate reports, automate processes, ensure consistency, measure KPI's, track progress, and collaborate on set of templates and processes built. However, they are of very limited value in managing human factors and the early stages of the design and build.

Scalability

PMO creation should be scalable; start small but be alert to the need to build on every component. Leverage the scalability model provided in early chapter as a guide to scalability criteria. The key to success is to start small and keep building till the desired state is reached starting from PMO setup, PMO processes, tools, and ending with staffing needs, and on-going sustainability plans.

Executive support
Executive buy-in and on-going support is pivotal to PMO longevity. The survey in chapter five shows how PMO's benefit from executive support. In the survey conducted as part of my PhD study, one of the questions was "what are the reasons for PMO failures?" to which one of the top three answers was "lack of Executive support".

Chapter Summary

In this chapter, the reader has been presented with the various types and models of PMO. Further, it covers the understanding between project, program, and portfolio PMO; the type of PMO authorities in the industry and the scalability models and their associated categories. Other functions such as PPM and QRM were covered and the overall PMOLC is introduced. The chapter ends with some PMO tips for the reader to consider.

CHAPTER 2

PMO SET-UP

The PMO set-up phase involves a seven step process. The chapter considers the set-up of a brand new PMO or the repurposing of an existing PMO; whether these are being completed as an internal project or with the help of external consultants. The set-up phase defines the organization's objectives in building a PMO in which are expressed as an approved PMO road map that describe the activities and steps required to build the PMO. This phase can be referred to as the identification or assessment phase. Identification in case of a new PMO (i.e. an organization never had a PMO) in which case all PMO elements are identified in order to establish the PMO roadmap; assessment in case of existing PMO (i.e. an organization that had a PMO and looking to revitalize its PMO), where all PMO elements are re-evaluated to confirm current elements, or identify changes required by the organization's leaders. Table 2.1 below summarizes the steps required to set-up a new PMO and an existing PMO. Each of these steps will be discussed in depth.

Table 2.1: PMOLC—Set-up Phase

PMO Set-up Steps	
New PMO	**Existing PMO**
Step 1: Identify the PMO sponsorship	**Step 1:** Assess current PMO sponsorship
Step 2: Identify PMO Type and Authority	**Step 2:** Assess effectiveness of current PMO Type and Authority
Step 3: Identify PMO Functions	**Step 3:** Assess current PMO Functions
Step 4: Identify PMO Staff	**Step 4:** Assess PMO Staff skill set
Step 5: Identify Project Managers Reporting Structure	**Step 5:** Assess current Project Managers Reporting Structure
Step 6: Identify PMO Interaction Model	**Step 6:** Assess effectiveness of current PMO interaction model
Step 7: Establish PMO Roadmap	**Step 7:** Re-establish PMO Roadmap

Newly created PMO

In previous chapters, we explored the PMO types and models; the differences in PMO authority and potential functions for every type. In this context, it is very important to understand the PMO reporting line because this will influence the set-up process.

Step 1: Identify the PMO sponsorship

In some cases, it may already be apparent to whom the PMO reports. In others, the head of the PMO or the expert involved is asked to assess where the PMO reporting line should be. To ensure success of PMO mandate, it is important to have a sponsor for the PMO that will support the PMO mission and resolve problems and facilitate resolutions.

Executives have several options for setting-up and building a PMO; they may choose to hire a full time team to create the PMO, with one internal executive champion to oversee the set-up of the PMO. Alternatively they may wish to invite a consultant to assess the PMO set-up and build-out, or hire new PMO experienced staff to build it. A third option is to employ an external specialist company who can set-up, build-out and run the PMO as a virtual PMO. There is no right or wrong approach;, all are viable options and it is important for the organization creating a PMO or the external entity assessing the organization for a PMO to understand the culture, the drivers for creating the PMO, expectations on it, and the elements of success required.

Internal hire:
Organizations may decide to hire a PMO subject matter expert as an internal resource to establish the PMO function, or promote some of the current project managers to help run the PMO function.

The advantage of this approach is that an internal project manager promoted into the role can help shorten the learning curve in terms of understanding the organization's culture and structure.

The disadvantage is that the skill set of the individual, who may be a high performing project manager, might not match that required to build a PMO. Even amongst those who build PMO's there are those who are, by nature, builders, and those that are operational. Ideally the two skills of build and operate should be combined. This though comes through years of experience in building PMOs and personal interest in doing both.

The PMO set-up can be projectized; however, the person working on the PMO set-up needs to have deeper skills than simply project management. Setting up a PMO requires someone who has worked at the senior level of an organization, understands strategy and planning, is well versed with organizations profit and loss, and has some number of years' experience in setting up PMO practices. If these skills are not found in someone within the organization, then the organization can either hire someone with these skills to lead the PMO set-up, or engage an external consulting firm who has experience.

External consulting:

Organizations may not have any experience in PMO set-up and build-out, and be unsure of what they should expect out of a PMO initially. Therefore, there is an advantage in inviting a consulting firm to assess the needs of the organization and provide the principal's organization with market perspective, education, and the requisite options. You may choose to use the assessment to understand better what benefits you can obtain from having a PMO, and hire someone to set-up and build it, or you may invite the consulting company to proceed with the set-up and build-out.

The main advantage in using consultants is the expertise they can provide which will help your executive team decide what is strategically and financially feasible; Another advantage of working with consultants is that it you to focus on the needs and issues within the organization while experts advise on the appropriate PMO set-up.

One real disadvantage when working with some consulting experts is that you may find the sheer volume of paperwork and analysis overwhelming. You need to manage expectations and oversee the consulting experts' delivery to ensure what you get is aligned with the needs of your organization and that your internal staff are trained to manage and operate the PMO after the consultants complete their work.

There are times when organizations need the rigor that a PMO can bring but has neither the capacity nor the skill set (and may not have the interest) to create a PMO, these organizations may opt for a Virtual PMO (i.e. outsourced PMO services) which is different from external consulting. While in external consulting, the final operationalization remains in the organizations hands, outsourced PMO operationalization is done by the vendor contracted to set-up, build, and run the day to day operation of the PMO. The next section discusses advantages of virtual PMOs and when that type of PMO is a viable option.

Virtual PMO:
The virtual PMO or what is referred to in the literature as outsourced PMO. Outsourcing is increasingly being employed to achieve performance improvements across the entire business. For example, one particular growth area has been the externalization of Information Technology (IT) with a recent report showing companies outsourcing 38% of their IT functions to external providers (McIvor, 2005).

Outsourcing has expanded beyond IT and manufacturing to include project management and project management offices. Many companies are already subscribing to Virtual PMO services which are the result of outsourcing services especially within IT which leads to PMOs in one geographic location servicing multiple others (Santosus, 2003).

A virtual PMO option has particular advantages when the PMO is outside of the core organizational functions, or the organization does not wish to take on full time employees to provide the PMO service. Some of these advantages are cost reduction for smaller organizations that do not wish to invest in infrastructure or resources. Another advantage is allowing organizations' internal resources to focus on core competencies and the ability to coordinate various skills and integrate them into multiple organization streams.

Some of the disadvantages of outsourcing is the reduction of staff in the main organization creating unemployment and transferring the jobs to the outsourcing partner, another disadvantage is the quality of work produced although some organization have gone around that and created service levels and strategic alliances to ensure quality expectations are met.

Step 2: Identify PMO type and authority

Chapter 1 explained the types of PMO and he authority associated with each. One of the first critical steps in establishing a PMO involves identifying the specific type of PMO and the functions associated with it. Arriving at this definition requires an assessment of the organization's culture as this will play an important part in the acceptance or rejection of the subsequent PMO. This assessment should consider how project management aligns with organizational strategy—in other words the role of project management within the business. It should also consider the level of organizational adaptability to change; the organization's priorities, and, most importantly the clarity of their goals and the correlation between these and the benefits of the PMO. BY way of example, table 2.2 below includes a compliance type PMO, its proposed PMO types and functions.

Given the decision to establish a PMO, an earlier assessment of the organization goals, should have identified the need for the PMO and the priorities it will need to address. For example, improving project delivery; or enabling better organization alignment of projects to organization goals across all departments; or improving consistency of work between functions, require an authoritative in nature PMO That authoritative PMO might be a division PMO reporting into a particular department (example an IT PMO, or product PMO), or it might be at the enterprise level that has oversight and authority to make decisions on staffing, processes, methodology and tools, as well as enforce compliance. To highlight this example, table 2.2 offers an example of PMO types and various functions they can run under an authoritative PMO.

Table 2.2: highlight the PMO type, and possible PMO functions under an authoritative PMO

PMO Authority	PMO Type	PMO Functions
Authoritative / Compliance	Project or Program	Project Methodology
	Division PMO	Project Processes
		Project Reporting
		Project Repository
	Enterprise PMO	Project Tools
	CoE PMO	Project Manager Development
		Project Delivery
	Global PMO	Project Portfolio

Step 3: Identify PMO functions

After identifying PMO sponsorship, the next step involves defining what functions are needed and the relative priority of these functions. Some functions need to be built sequentially while others can be built in parallel. Example for sequential function build is project methodology. There is a need to have the methodology in place before training project managers to use it. Example of parallel function build is while building project delivery process, reporting capabilities can be built at the same time.

Step 4: Identify PMO staff

Identifying PMO staffing needs should be done from both a short and long term perspective. PMO will eventually need a mix of roles such as project analysts, process analysts, portfolio analysts, project tools specialists, project, and program managers. For a start, a PMO leader needs to be identified either by direct hiring, through internally promoting senior program managers, portfolio managers, or consulting to experts who are knowledgeable in project management offices set-up. Immediate need of resources will be a process and methodology specialist to help either build or support the processes and methodologies needed in the early stages. In later stage, as the breadth of projects is identified, more project managers need to be hired, and a project tool specialist who can support project managers in the use of tools and generate required KPI's.

Step 5: Identify project managers' reporting structure

This step requires understanding the organization landscape. Should project managers report into the business units only, or should they report into the PMO only, or a mix of both. Chapter 6, survey question reports that 30% of organizations project managers' reported into the PMO, while other % split between business and PMO in different variations. To determine best reporting structure, need to ask organization leaders where do they believe better alignment will be, ask the project managers were do they fit from career advancement, and understand PMO's type, then determine where the project managers reporting structure should be. Smaller organization tend to have project managers within the PMO because they are too small to spread the project managers, while larger organization have a mix of project managers reporting into the PMO and these work on the larger, cross-functional projects, while the business units project managers work the departmental projects that are contained within the business unit.

Step 6: Identify the PMO Interaction Model

It is important to understand how the new function of PMO will interact with the rest of the organization. Some functions may view the PMO as competition; threatening to take away responsibilities or authority, or dictate work processes. Setting the right expectations and identifying the interactions between the PMO and other business units facilitates better adoption of the PMO. Other functions understand how the PMO will work and interact with other functional departments.

For every interaction, there are inputs, and outputs expected from each party that can be summarized in figure 2.1 below. For example, PMO requires input from every business unit the list of their initiatives; in return, the PMO output a consolidated list of all organization's initiative. Another example, business units input resources to staff a project, the output from PMO is resource allocation and potential resource constraint. The output from the PMO can be used as input to the business units to reassign resources, and re-prioritize workload to achieve resource allocation balance.

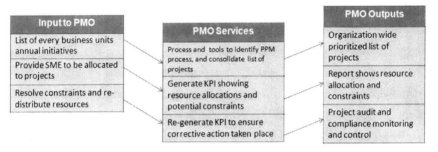

Figure 2.1 Sample of PMO services and its relevant outputs to other business units

Step 7: Establish the PMO roadmap

This step can only occur after all previous steps have been completed. The PMO roadmap should include all the assessment of the current state, identify gaps in capabilities and impact of these gaps, and offer a proposals for solutions related to identified gaps. A word of caution: a PMO roadmap is bespoke to a given organization; there may be useful elements and features that you can glean from other organizations and their experience of the PMO function. However, there is no generic blueprint for this process. The PMO road map should detail the structure of the PMO, the type, model, various functions to be built for short term and long term. It is also important to establish the required reporting structure for supporting staff and project managers, and define how the new function will interact with other existing functions. The road map, once approved, will become the source for enabling the plan through build-out and then execution. For a copy of an example PMO roadmap, refer to appendix B.

Existing PMO

Some PMOs grow stale and they stop adding value, or the value declines and the PMO leaders or the PMO sponsor need to step back and assess what went wrong and take corrective action. If assessment is done frequently, organization may avoid drastic overhauls to their PMO, but often when these assessments are neglected, we often get PMO's being shut down, transformed, or marginalized. Therefore, the steps for the existing PMO are meant to go over the PMO authority, functions established, project managers reporting structure, and effectiveness of current PMO interaction of the organization. It can start by creating a survey getting the pulse of the organization an dif the feedback is marginal or folks are generally satisfied with the PMO, then no changes are required, but if the results are not positive, then the assessment is required. The checking the pulse of the organization should be structured standard frequent practice.

Step 1: Assess the current PMO Sponsorship

An organization may already be running one or more PMO's. The assessment outcome may call for consolidation of PMOs that might be redundant, or improve current alignment between the existing PMOs. Taking corrective action along with the organization changes is the accountability of the PMO sponsor who needs to champion the flow of information to inform PMO of change in direction.

Assessing the current sponsorship is important to know whether the PMO still has the support it needs to be vital organization. Sometime there are changes in the directions of the organization or to the role of the sponsor that may impact PMO support negatively. PMO sponsor must be effective at all times by providing organization feedback to PMO leaders to continue improving and by supporting PMOs mission in the organization, and if strategic direction change the way PMO should operate, the PMO leader needs to be aware to make the adjustment required. In absence of direction and guidance (i.e. sponsorship), PMO can become stale and disconnected from organization leaders. There are times when aligning with the current sponsor might not be good for the longevity of the PMO due to organizational changes; hence, PMO leader must be front and center rallying for sponsorship at the executive committees to ensure proper alignment and support is there.

Step 2: Assess effectiveness of current PMO Type and Authority

The objective in this assessment is to determine if the current PMO type and level of authority is still effective or not, and if not what is the proposed action plan. The assessment can happen through hiring external consultant to get a neutral view to the organization and in that case they need the PMO roadmap that was established. In absence of one, they need to survey the organization executives and those that the PMO support and provide services to. The assessment can be internal assessment, where the PMO lead can play the survey part and gauge with his audience if the PMO as it is today still a viable function or not. If the answer that changes need to be made, then the recommendation should provide what type of PMO the current PMO need to transfer to and what authority changes need to be made. For example upon assessment the outcome might be that the authority given to the PMO is that making the PMO more like a cop and authority to scrutinize all work efforts, and that is creating animosity atmosphere, then the PMO need to look into becoming more consultative, or more of a coach. The opposite maybe true and the results show PMO is not enforcing some of the standards and requires the PMO to take more authority tone towards enforcing standards through rewards, and consequences measures.

Step 3: Assess the current PMO functions

All the current PMO functions need to be reviewed against the original expectations. The assessing party external or internal need to compare actual to plan and what is anticipated of each function. For example, if the PMO road map called for three functions: process development, project managers training, and project reporting. The assessment should look at if these functions exist and if they do how they are performing currently. If one of the functions was looked over for example project managers training, it will have an impact on adopting the processes, and reporting accurately and this may impact negatively the PMO performance. There might be times where the current functions are working as expected, but a need to expand into new areas such as developing automated capabilities to allow teams to collaborate, or mechanism to prioritize projects which indicative of readiness of the organization to take on more through having the PMO expand and perform the next set of expected functions that may not necessarily were in the roadmap, or were as phase two, which this current assessment might be expediting.

Step 4: Assess PMO staff skill set

Full assessments to all PMO staff need to take place to determine performance of each individual, and skill set gap across the same level, and across the various levels. In order to achieve this assessment, first, an inventory of current staff skill sets (along with their aspirations), looking for evidence of their past performance and of professional development and assess if they have been delivering as expected against the role expectations and relevant to PMO roadmap requirements. Second, validating whether the number of staff supporting the PMO is sufficient, and whether the skill set available is diverse enough to address the different types of projects. The result of this assessment is rewarding performing staff, and taking corrective action of those who are not performing as well. The assessment will further result in defining the job family for project managers and PMO staff as well as highlight the career path progression. Employee satisfaction is an area if not assessed frequently; PMO will risk staff turn around and stability of performing employees.

Step 5: Assess current project managers reporting structure

While step 4 recommended assessing project managers' individual skills, step 5 step requires a completely objective assessor to determine the current reporting structure effectiveness. The reason for a third part assessor is that PMO lead might be bias towards having the project managers report into the PMO, while other leaders with their diverged agendas would keep project managers reporting into their functions. An organization may have started with all project managers reporting into the PMO, others may have started that project managers report into their business units. Some organizations have hybrid models were by some project managers' report into the PMO while others report into their business units. The assessment of already established PMO needs to take place to either confirm current established structure, or change the structure if required. An indicator to the structure would be is the organization centralized around business unit, if each unit has their supporting technology, and other services, then the expectations will be to have project managers' report into them. If the organization is specialty focused by which every department is focused on delivering their products and good and project managers are supporting cross functional initiatives, then a centralized project manager s reporting into the PMO is more appropriate. At any point if the structure shifts, assessment of project managers reporting structure need to be re-visited to ensure what type of alignment would be more effective.

Step 6: Assess effectiveness of current PMO interaction model

In this step, the assessment of interaction model effectiveness should be under review in an existing PMO. The assessment will include going through all inputs, outputs and defined interactions with other business units and validating whether the practice in place is valid or it requires an update. Sometimes, there are organization transformations that introduces new business unit or eliminate business units, this impacts the PMOs interaction with these new business unit and PMO will risk effective support if the services are assumed and looked into carefully.

Step 7: Re-establish PMO roadmap

The PMO roadmap involves documenting all the assessments and all the results to establish the guidance to carry on and execute. The objective of the assessment is not to carry out the work, but more to ensure agreement on the assessment results and confirm required changes. The difference in this roadmap from the newly developed PMO is that the roadmap resulting for assessing an existing PMO need to take in consideration the current practice, identify the gaps, and recommend an execution plan (i.e. an action plan) that gets carried out in the build-out phase.

Chapter Summary

In this chapter, the reader has been presented with the PMO set-up steps. The seven steps to set-up a new PMO and steps to address existing PMO.

CHAPTER 3

PMO BUILD-OUT

The build-out phase will, by definition, depend on the success of the delivery of the set-up phase. The set-up phase can be treated as planning the work; while the build-out phase is executing on the planned work. Since PMO helps the organization structure projects, and deliver them; the PMO build-out need to be planned and executed as if it is a project. The complexity of the PMO build-out is that although it needs to be treated like a project, you will also need an operational plan as part of the project plan. In other words, as PMO functions are being rolled out, you should already have a plan and be taking actions to support its on-going improvement, support, and sustainability in the organization. The journeys of set-up and build-out of the PMO are not discrete but ongoing processes. The table below summarizes the steps required to build-out a new or re-establish an existing PMO. Each step will be further explored.

Table 3.1: PMOLC—Build-out Phase

PMO Build-out Steps	
New PMO	**Existing PMO**
Step 1: Create PMO execution plan	Step 1: Create PMO execution plan
Step 2: Build Methodology	Step 2: Update Methodology
Step 3: Build Processes	Step 3: Update Processes
Step 4: Implement Tools	Step 4: Improve Tools effectiveness
Step 5: Build Other PMO functions	Step 5: Re-align Other PMO functions
Step 6: Build Interaction model	Step 6: Re-vitalize Interaction model
Step 7: Build Governance model	Step 7: Improve standard and governance model

Newly created PMO

Step 1: Create the PMO execution plan

This is the first step in the build-out phase which links to the roadmap that was the output of last step in the set-up phase. While the roadmap depicts the blueprint for a PMO build-out of an organization, the execution plan depicts the implementation plan with all the activities that needs to be identified. Execution plan identify how these components will be built and the timeframe it will take to complete, validate the resource needs and manage the cost of the build-out. As the execution plan is taking place, as part of executive status reporting, the head of the PMO must always confirm direction and validity of what is being delivered with the PMO sponsor and Executive team that have funded and supported the existence of the PMO. The head of the PMO must have insight to the changes going on within his/ her organization and how that may impact the PMO build-out. Organization executives must also be aware of any new industry trends and challenges that could affect PMO implementation positively or negatively. For example, if the organization is building a PMO that had consolidated business functions as part of realignment and organization transformation, it will impact the interaction model of the PMO which needs to be revisited to determine of what was documented in the setup-up either still holds, or needs to be changed.

Step 2: Build Methodology

The overall goal of building methodology is to provide consistent and standardized methods for the project lifecycle in terms of how projects are planned, executed, monitored, and closed. Further, establish governing policies and procedures required for a PMO to measure and ensure compliance. One of the core roles of a PMO is to establish and adopt a standard methodology that contains all the required templates, and guidance, to allow improved project delivery.

In newly established PMO and depending on where the PMO reports into, the PMO may need to develop and support a number of methodologies. Starting with an industry standard project framework, such as PMI's 5 process areas (initiation, planning, execution, control, and close) will offer significant benefits. Having an industry standard will save "re-inventing the wheel", and offers an industry benchmark against which the organization can measure itself.

Templates need to be developed only after methodology has been selected to ensure alignment with the methodology requirements. Starting small is a major win, many PMOs try too much, too fast, and end up stumbling on rollout and measuring results, and it takes longer to wait on all methodologies to be in place to start executing. A tip for those building methodologies to build essential foundation, then build on it for success, ensure pilot group implementation especially for large organizations were not to disrupt projects that are in-flight. An operation plan / action plan needs to be in place to ensure what is being built can be used and consumed and can be measured as well. A focus on the use of templates and their content, the quality and applicability of the templates and their contents with frequent revisions for updates corresponding to processes and procedures changes.

Step 3: Build processes

The overall goal of building processes is to complement the methodologies in place, and to provide a step by step instruction on how to go about using and running the methodologies in place. An organization may end with set of processes complementing the many methodologies of choice. For example, if an organization using PMI methodology, the process will be different for an organization ITPMO in nature that chooses to adopt RUP. One of the roles of PMO is to build processes and their associated procedures, and sub-procedures. For example, the process for change management should include what type of changes are documented, the template to hold the change, the escalation procedure including iterations, reviews, sign-offs associated with it.

An operation plan / action plan needs to be in place to ensure what is being built can be used and consumed and can be measured as well, more in-depth discussion on operationalizing processes will be covered in the sustainability chapter.

Step 4: Implement Tools

The overall goal of implementing project and portfolio tools is to automate and support the methodology and process adoption through the implementation of tools that will support portfolio management and project management efforts. PMO's role in portfolio and project management tools implementation would be to define, implement directly or through vendors, coordinate internal efforts, train organization and pilot the tools before mass rollout, and finally plan the ongoing operation of tools for portfolio, project and resource management.

There are baseline and standards requirements that must be achieved to determine what work is required (this include technology needs from hardware, software, and license), and how it will be performed (this refer to the configuration and how much of the tool will be used, when, planning all activities in a project schedule). Having proven that processes and methodologies are in place is a key to successful tools implementation; although not mandatory. Many tools today are at an advanced level for project and portfolio that can be used as a catalyst to change within an organization and yet better may change the way business is done (i.e. influence process alignment, enhancement, and/or a change).

Two assessments will need to be performed. One, identify the readiness of the organization project management processes, maturity of the methodology, and requirements established to the benefits desired out of the tool. Second, identify requirements pertaining to resources (hardware, software, infrastructure, network, and security), type of tool since there are variety in the market, and finally the on-going operation support. Whether the work will be performed internally or externally to the organization, SME with expertise in tools deployment and processes alignment are keys to successful implementation and assurance to smooth on-going operation support. Example of well-known tool include MS Project a widely known project scheduling tool, in addition to other collaboration tools, like Enterprise risk management, reporting tools, and document repository, etc. These tools should be flexible and serve the various organizational needs. Some organization may choose to implement and host the solutions with supporting staff from technology and vendors. Other organizations may choose a SAAS (Software as a service) model which allows organization that doesn't have capacity to have their solution supported by a third party. Some influences on internal vs. external hosting decisions organizations take often depends on their security, budget, structure, and resources.

Step 5: Build Other PMO functions

This step executes the functions that have been identified during the set-up phase in addition the main functions shown in the steps above, process, methodology, tools. Further, it builds what other functions the PMO is required to build and in what time frame. For example if one of the required functions is the project manager development, then the PMO head must identify the inputs and outputs as in table 3.2 below. Further, execute on the development plan by improving baseline skills set, progressing project managers career, and retaining them through work assignments that reward their professional advancement.

Table 3.2: Example of PMO function inputs and expected output

Project Manager Development Function	
Function Inputs	Function Outputs
Skill set assessment tools to benchmark skills	Project managers skills benchmark
Organization goals	Career path and project culture
Current project management opportunities	Assignments based on skill set
Salary analysis compared to market standards	Competitive compensation relevant to skills

The overall goal is to encourage continued development and improvement in the core skills and competencies of project managers to achieve a higher performance, thus helping to ensure a successful project management career path. The PMO's role for people is to build a career path for project and program managers by defining required competency profiles at the various maturity levels of a project manager. Additionally, the development of the PMO's capabilities can help determine how the PMO can use these profiles to evaluate and predict performance of all project and program managers as part of an organization's annual appraisals.

An assessment of the Project Managers' skills can be achieved through understanding their background, their current work assignments, and their previous project management experience, certifications, interests, career goals, etc. Whether through structured meetings, surveys, or questionnaires, or even a combination of these approaches, an organization should establish an inventory of its human assets. This assessment will provide an understanding of the strengths and weakness of each individual, and provide the organization with the necessary information to determine the areas for improvement and the methods that needs to be taken to increase the individual's skill level so as to improve project performance. Once an assessment is completed, the PMO produces an operation plan for improvement.

Step 6: Build interaction model

While in the set-up, the interaction model should have been identified. This step ensures that the interaction model is implemented and acted upon. The build-out task is to execute on the defined model and ensures that the flow of information and services from each and every business unit into and out of the PMO including all inputs and outputs are happening per the agreed upon interaction. For example, PMO interacting with the Finance business unit, will need input on annual project portfolio budget allocation, classification whether its capital and expense. The PMO and Finance would collaborate on classification of these initiatives in terms of organization ranking, resources requirements (internal, external), and Financial constraints, and the timeliness of PMO reporting. The outputs from the PMO consist of project financial control on actual spend in terms of hours and cost, priority of execution, and whether projects have been cancelled or terminated to assess financial benefit realization. For a detailed copy of the interaction model template, refer to appendix A

Step 7: Build governance model

The overall goal of a establishing a governance model is to provide organization transparency to the decisions being made. Governance structure ensures that directions are provided to guide the decisions need to be made, who is responsible for making these decisions and the process of approval or hierarchy that is required to ensure a decision was made after all appropriate level of reviews were made. Governance is defined as the creation of a project's organizational structure (Carver, 2000).

Doughty & Grieco (2005) use the term "governance" generally referring to control processes and procedures used to both control and direct the actions of an organization and to determine who is held to account for these actions. Selig & Waterhouse (2006) It is this collection of management, planning and review processes, as well as the associated decision rights that enables the organization to determine and establish performance metrics thus formalizing and clarifying their responsibilities of oversight and accountability. Klagegg et.al (2008) shows that establishing governance frameworks are important to securing transparency and control and clarify the role of the sponsor.

Governance, as it applies to projects should be structured in a way that aids the organization decision making pertaining to projects. The flow of information regarding status, issues, accomplishments, and outstanding should be guided through defined layers as in the example in figure 3.1 below which shows at the bottom, the most fundamental layer the project delivery which consists of project work streams lead by project managers, leading to the middle tier which may consist of the PMO, the project steering committee(s), and organization product or service delivery in charge. Then, in the top tier, a representation at the organization level depicted by strategic oversight which may represent the C-level in some organization or other senior executives that may consist of various boards.

Figure 3.1 Conceptual model of Possible Project Governance model within an organization

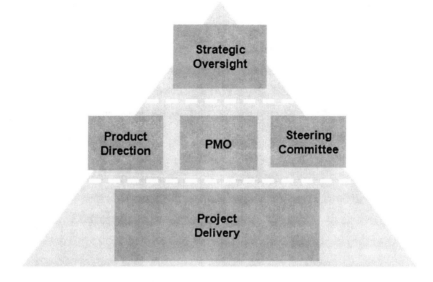

Existing PMO

Step 1: Create PMO execution plan

This is the first step in the build-out phase which links to the roadmap that was the output of last step in the set-up phase. While the roadmap depicts the blueprint for a PMO build-out of an organization, the execution plan depicts the implementation plan with all the activities that needs to be carried out. Execution plan identify how these components will be built and the timeframe it will take to complete these activities, validate the resource needs and manage the cost of the build-out. While execution is taking place and the various functions being built and staffed, the head of the PMO must always confirm the validity of what is being delivered with the PMO sponsor and Executive team that have funded and supported the existence of the PMO. The head of the PMO must have insight to the changes going on within his/her organization and how that may impact the PMO implementation. They must also be aware of any new industry trends and challenges that could affect PMO implementation positively or negatively. For example, if the organization building a PMO had consolidated some business function as part of an overall realignment and organization transformation, it will impact the interaction model of the PMO and the activities between these functions and PMO will need to be revisited to determine the deviation from what was documented in the setup-up phase.

This first step involves ensuring that the outputs from the PMO reassessment in the set-up phase has been approved, and agreements on updates and changes have been clearly confirmed. A New implementation plan is needed to carry out all the approved activities. There is no different in terms of the structure and expectations from the execution plan perspective between a newly established PMO and an existing. While in the newly established PMO, the execution plan is laying the foundation and building a function, in the existing PMO its changing a particular practice by adding, changing, or eliminating a component.

Step 2: Update methodology

This first step involves ensuring that a standard methodology is in place. Then an assessment is required to determine whether the current methodology that is in place is sufficient for what is needed to be accomplished, or if the assessment outcome is that the methodology used is not the right methodology, maybe it is more appropriate to re-build the methodology.

For example if a PMO had a mandate to build an organization methodology which in this case PMI PMBOK, and the role of the PMO had expanded to include IT delivery and a new methodology such as Agile was required. The PMO need to take on the methodology if it already in place and assess embedding the various methodologies and how will it support that. For example, if Agile is what is requested, but have not been implemented, it is a bigger task because on one hand the PMO need to look at implementing the new methodology and follow steps of a new build-out of a methodology, and on the other hand, the PMO still needs to assess how to manage the suite of methodologies going forward and mechanism in place to support each methodology. The outcome may result in Agile SME, resources to build and support the new methodology, training for IT staff on the new methodology, and expanding resources to support and coach in agile methods.

Step 3: Update Processes

In this step, after assessment of process group gaps, the changes and updates to these processes should be identified, prioritized, and implemented. PMO should be the place that houses the processes that capture the information flow and describe the steps to executing a work flow. Example of main process areas that needs to be examined are: Risk management process, Lessons learned process, Change management processes. For example if the change management process to be updated, an assessment to 1—whether change management is formally documented and relevant templates and guidance are available, 2—whether it is followed and adhered to, 3—identify the gaps in the documenting of the process or in following the process and whether lack of following the change management process is due to lack of education and understanding or whether it is resistance to following processes. Depending on the assessment an action plan needs to be in place to address these gaps which may require executive support in enforcing compliance with the set standards, or it may be simply more education and training on the use and expectation for the change management process.

Step 4: Improve tools effectiveness

In this step, assessment of current tools is required to take place after assessment of processes to ensure that change in the process will impact the tools usage, and not the other way around change in tools capabilities would result in a process group gaps. Tools improvement happens in two ways:

- First, the way the tool is configured for use, is it too tightly integrated with the processes; hence, the magnitude of flexibility is lost and as a result changes in the tools are disruptive and discouraged. The opposite might be true and that is the tool is open ended without any protocols, policies and procedures that govern the checks and balances of its use and standards and conformance to standards can be an issue.
- Second, the way the tools are being used to generate effective reports, risks, issues, timesheets, resource demands, etc. There are a large number of tools in the market and each has its advantages and disadvantages. A great advantage would be a tool or tools set that integrate and interface with other applications and with the organization processes. Assessments of the current tools in use are a key to understand and fully explore tools' capabilities to be able to extend, expand, or build upon.

Step 5: Re-align other PMO functions

This step defines how other functions if they exist would line up with the methodology, process, and tools. For example, if the project manager development function existed, the PMO should ensure a regular and on-going assessment is performed. An assessment of the Project Managers' skills can be achieved through understanding their background, their current work assignments, and their previous project management experience, certifications, interests, career goals, etc. Whether through structured meetings, surveys, or questionnaires, or even a combination of these approaches, an organization should establish an inventory of its human assets. This assessment will provide an understanding of the strengths and weakness of each individual, and provide the organization with the necessary information to determine the areas for improvement and the methods that needs to be taken to increase the individual's skill level so as to improve project performance.

If the function doesn't exist, it might be prudent to look into creating it to ensure if it fits in the current PMO structure, organizational culture, and funding support required for the PMO. Similarly, other functions within the PMO needs to be assessed and may require realignment if these functions exist and re-assessment if they should be introduced as a result of PMO expansion, evolution, or improvement needs to be considered. For example, a PMO might be missing on reporting which means reports have to be established and understanding of KPI's to allow the various layers of the organization to make decision. Another example, a PMO might be missing transparency or visualization of some reports, maybe the reports go to executives but not to senior directors below the executive level, or completely vise versa. As a result, realignment of the reporting function requires identifying who needs these reports, when do they need it, and what decisions and actions result from going through it. Once an assessment is completed, the PMO produces an operation plan for continuous improvement.

Step 6: Re-vitalize interaction model

This step is to re-visit the current interaction model in place. First, an assessment of whether the interaction model in place has been active and the PMO has been operating based on the defined (inputs, outputs, and required elements in place). Two, if the interactions and collaborations between all business units and PMO have been taken place according to the documented interactions, and that any required changes due to organizational change has been reflected and acted upon. In either case, the assessment will determine how wide or narrow is the gap between interaction flow and current inputs and outputs. If a gap exists, then a plan is required to address the re-vitalization exercise where buy-in from other departments is vital. Approval on interactions and commitments, and accountability exchanges is a key success to PMO for a healthy relation in an organization.

Step 7: Improve standards and governance model

This step is to re-visit current governance model. It includes build-out of policies, procedures, and revitalization of current templates based on organizational dynamics and consistent with the established organizational structure and culture. Standards and governance should work hand in hand with standards built and governance should enforce the standards. Some of the questions that need to be asked are:

- Are there performance standards in place?
- Are the performance measures adequate?
- Is the existing governance model supports and enforces the set standards?

If the answer is no, to any of these questions, then standards need to be either redefined, or measures needs to be addressed. Maybe the issue is not in the set standards but maybe in the authority to enforce these standards (i.e. the governance). Governance model needs to take into consideration enforcing the organization standards even if it means changing bad habits and dealing with behavioral issues, the PMO should have executive support to set the standards and ability to enforce them.

Chapter Summary

In this chapter, the reader has been presented with the PMO build-out steps. The seven steps to build-out a new PMO or to address an existing PMO.

CHAPTER 4

PMO SUSTAINABILITY

As the build-out phase depends on the success or the delivery of the set-up phase. Similarly the sustainability phase is dependent on the success of the build-out phase. The success in creating a function or a department is in the longevity of that function and the value this function adds through day to day operation to ensure sustainability. The journey of setting up and building a PMO is half of the work; the rest of the work is in operationalizing these functions with day to day work ensuring continuous improvement plans leading to sustainability of the PMO organization.

Sustainability Principles

The author will explore what it means for a PMO to sustain operation and continue the improvement journey. PMO's are concerned with delivering the right projects and delivering these projects right. For that to happen PMO needs to have a plan demonstrating to its executive sponsors and its broader organization that improvements are throughout time.

Sustainability principles call for social-oriented, economical, and ecological systems. These systems can be for midterm or long term and can span from local to global. Most notable is the notion of value-base, which is considered the foundation for sustainable project management (Gareis et. al, 2011). Another definition for PMO that emphasizes value add as defined by the author

> *PMO is a critical organizational entity that adopts a variety of roles and structures but should be focused on adding value to an organization and its customers to achieve the desired organizational performance.* (karkukly, 2010, p. 55)

From the PMO definition above, PMO should be contributing to add value to its organization and the organizations it services, i.e. the customers' organizations. A more formal definition of value-add is that

> *Value added refers to "extra" feature(s) of an item of interest (product, service, person etc.) that go beyond the standard expectations and provide something "more" while adding little or nothing to its cost.* (wikipedia.org/wiki/Value_add)

Bowman and Ambrosini introduce two dimensions to value add. First, the human resources as a dimension of an organization and how employee performance can attribute to organization profit/success. Second, value capture based on customer perception of the received value (Bowman and Ambrosini, 2000).

To focus on establishing value-add dimensions, the human resources value add and the customer value add will be explored along with the various elements that ensure sustainability in each dimension. Further consideration will be given to the risk management factors that influences the customer and HR value-add measures.

Human Resources value

Following Maslow's theory, human resources are motivated differently depending on what stage of value hierarchy which can be summarized into food, shelter, social, economical, and finally self actualization of having a self purpose. Employers are motivated through financial and through self-fulfillment through challenging assignments, employer's respect, and career progression. Ultimately to generate performance improvement with individuals, they need to be motivated; this motivation reflect in improving their work by minimizing issues, and improving efficiencies leading to continuous improvements that, involves HR factors, portfolio factors, and delivery factors which are described below

Human Resource factor

- Trusting employees to share organization leaders' goals
- Empowering employees to execute on these goals
- Improving their skill sets
- Promoting and rewarding for value add work

Portfolio factor (Initiative alignment)

- Align and prioritize initiative based on organization's value
- Define projects with value add criteria
- Communicate the value add to the organization
- Embed the value add (especially for project base organization) into goals and objectives

Delivery factor

- Improve estimation through standardization
- Monitor and control scope and schedule

- Identify delivery success criteria as seen by the organization leads
- Identify value add from delivery as seen by customers

Figure 4.1 HR Value factors

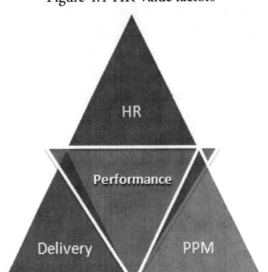

An example of combining HR factor, delivery, and portfolio leading to performance success would start in ensuring the human resource aspect is provided with the tools and standards required to help them. Investing in training the project managers in the project management profession as well as on the job, and allowing these project managers to lead projects from the portfolio that align with their skills and experience. Hold these project managers accountable to using the set standards in place, and in absence of it reward those who standardize and facilitate the work for the project team. Embed the value-add measures within a project by identifying what is required from these project managers on their projects to consider the project successful (i.e. identify success criteria of what is considered as meets expectation, exceed expectation, or below expectation means) Embed these measures into their performance evaluation stating the reward in case of meeting or exceeding expectations, as well as penalties from not meeting these measures. This is not a one-time exercise, improving on it and reflecting on how to better motivate the human resource dimension reflect in continuous improvements for the PMO and increase the performance for the individuals and of the function.

Customer value

(Michael Treacy and Fred Wiersema) have developed a model that defines leading companies and their relation with their customers which focuses on three types of disciplines and these are:

- *Customer intimacy*: being very close to the voice of the customer and have intimate knowledge of their needs which drive customized solutions to each that gain their loyalty.
- *Operational excellence*: focus on providing customers with combination of quality and low price and be able to maintain services 365 days a year.
- *Product leadership*: Achieved though innovation and development of products that elevate performance limits. (Hoque et al., 2005)

PMO will need to align with its organization on the type of customer value model its organization to satisfy. To be able to quantify the value-add, there are quantitative and qualitative measures to customer value. Quantitative can be achieved through customer relationship and measuring their satisfaction through customer surveys, meetings, one-on-one, and town hall meetings that address wider customer needs. Qualitative can be achieved through ensuring that the company is customer focused and these customers are receiving quality factor, the time delivery factor, and cost factor as described below

Quality Factor

- Ensure delivery of product or service is error free
- Ensure quality measures and improvements are in place
- Ensure commitment to quality when issues arise

Delivery factor

- Receive product and service on time
- Submit requests to change on time
- Communicate delivery success criteria to set right expectation
- Identify value add from delivery

Cost Factor
- Receive cost effective product or service
- Ensure the cost of running product and service is competitive
- Value is demonstrated through cost but on fixing errors or improving current offering
- Assess cost of changes and improvement in product or service

Figure 4.2 Customer Value factors

An example of combining quality factor, delivery factor, and cost factor leading to customer satisfaction would start in setting and communicating the right expectations with the customer. Over-promising and under-delivering would impact the delivering organization reputation. Delivering a product with errors and unavailability of timely support will jeopardize the relation and will lead to unsatisfied client. Being competitive on cost and ensuring that the organization customer is getting more value out of the product or service relative to the cost that will give that customer a competitive edge in their market. PMO that understand how to improve in its sustainability journey will understand these three customer value factors and will ensure immediate focus on them whether the customer internal to the organization, external, or both. Improving timeliness of delivery, quality of delivery, and monitor and control the cost are key areas that PMO would help its organization in achieving a value-add services that reflect in customer satisfaction.

Risk Management Factor

It is prudent to give further consideration to the risk management factors because they have impacts on the HR and customer value-add measures either negatively or positively. While positive impact will be received well, nevertheless, organization should document the triggers and outcomes to ensure repeatability. The negative impact however needs to be carefully considered through identification and analysis of these risks and having a plan to addressing them in order to sustain the HR and customer value-add. First, the focus will be on the risk factors that will below are the risk factors that influence the HR and customer value and these risks are:

HR Risk Factors

- Business Model Risk: Ensure that PMO model in place is robust and address organizational needs

- Alignment Risk: Ensure alignment of project resources to the set processes and standards regardless whether they report into the PMO or not
- Integration Risk: Ensure integration of processes across the organization through understanding current interaction model
- Governance Risk: Ensure governance that ensure timely flow of information and enables timely decision making

Customer Risk Factors

- Competitive risk: Providing product or service that is leader in its kind offering the customer organization and product organization with the competitive advantage in the market
- Investment risk: Ensure investments in products and services align with customer needs and that outcome is cost competitive
- Governance Risk: Ensure governance in place through CRM and SLA to improve response back and ensure timely information are reached from and to the customer's organization. It is important to make a note that internal governance should be structured in a way that is foundation for customer governance and that one does not conflict with the other.

Second focus will be on the risk triggers that are associated with these factors and these are summarized below in two categories identification and action taken. Regardless of what risk factor, the risk identification and action plan process will be similar.

Risk identification triggers

- Ensure that risks are identified, classified, and prioritized
- Assess and address the risks and assign a severity and impact as in low, medium, high

- Know whether the impact on the HR or customer value-add and whether it is direct, indirect

Risk undertaking

- Define alternatives to address the risk and their impact
- Define mechanism for escalation and reporting
- Take action and execute to ensure minimal impact to HR and customer value-add

Figure 4.3 Summary of value-add dimensions, factors, and influencing triggers

Value-add Dimensions	Value Factors	Risk Factors
Human Resource	➢ HR ➢ Portfolio ➢ Delivery	✓ Business Model ✓ Alignment ✓ Integration ✓ Governance
Customer	➢ Quality ➢ Delivery ➢ Cost	✓ Competitiveness ✓ Investment ✓ Governance

Risk Triggers
Risk Identification
Risk Action taking

PMO Sustainability

The sustainability phase involves a seven step process from start to completion. The process considers the sustainability after or during a build-out of a brand new PMO or the takes into consideration the sustainability of an existing PMO. This phase can be referred to as the operationalization phase, on-going support, or continuous improvement Table 4.1 below summarizes the steps required to sustain a PMO. Each of these steps will be discussed in depth.

Table 4.1: PMOLC—Sustainability

PMO Sustainability Steps	
New PMO	**Existing PMO**
Step 1: Sustain reporting performance	**Step 1:** Re-align reporting performance
Step 2: Sustain support of PMO tools	**Step 2:** Re-align support of PMO tools
Step 3: Sustain training and mentoring programs	**Step 3:** Re-align training and mentoring programs
Step 4: Sustain PMO Staff skills and structure	**Step 4:** Re-align PMO Staff skills and structure
Step 5: Sustain executive commitments	**Step 5:** Re-align executive commitments
Step 6: Sustain continuous feedback loop	**Step 6:** Re-establish continuous feedback loop
Step 7: Sustain improvement action plan	**Step 7:** Re-establish improvement action plan

Newly created PMO

Step 1: Sustain reporting performance

This step assumes that reporting function have been built already. There are two elements to any effective PMO reporting function:

1. *Process,* in other words how often and when are reports generated, what form do they take, who receives them and how do the reports influence the organizations decision-making processes and how do they enable action? A focus on measuring the process itself and how it is being followed to achieve the end result; assessing its level of complexity and adapting the right action to ensure its effectiveness.

2. *Content,* what data do you need to capture and why and how are your presenting it?
   Projects are notorious for the amount of data they generate so you should spend time finding ways of streamlining information on the project statues with an appropriate dashboard for executives and well-considered KPIs. Since organizations and

their requirements change, KPI's cannot be one size fits all; therefore, there is a need to anticipate mechanisms for changing and adapting organization reporting function and platforms too as required

For PMO to achieve continuous improvements, KPI's need to be presenting various details and levels of information catering to all organization layers, detailed KPI's when needed, and high level KPI's at other times, striking a balance is through identifying initial reporting needs, and more so ability to keep up updating it based on the evolving needs.

Step 2: Sustain support of PMO tools

This step assumes that project and portfolio tools have been built already. There are two elements to any effective PMO tools support function:

1. *Usability*, in other words provide project managers, team members, PMO administrators with ease of use and ability to interact in and out of the system with minimal system issues. User friendly interfaces that allow casual users with the ability to pull the right information, interact and prioritize, and collaborate at all levels. Tools usability is correlated with the level of adoption of these tools. The easier the tool to be use and navigate, or the availability of guide and support increase the use of it, the opposite is true.

2. *Stability*, the ability to maximize tools uptime and improve operation support are two important elements to ensure stability, this is includes: hardware capacity, network bandwidth, security access, availability, etc. Other components such as scheduling system maintenance, outages, and upgrades outside of core

work hours to minimize interruptions. Further, learning when to turn tools features on as users of the system mature in their practice is a key to ensuring stability.

As organization reporting needs evolve, the need for robust tools becomes important. For example, as needs of analytical reporting increase, the PMO will need a robust tool for gathering business intelligence and trend data about the project and program function and the general performance of the business over time. A key to success lies in integrating current tools into a comprehensive delivery framework, and assessing additional tools if needed to improve project performance.

Step 3: Sustain training and mentoring programs

Step 4: Sustain PMO staff skills and structure

The two steps are combined for the overlap they have. While step 3 considers the on-going training programs, the types of training, and producing training programs at the various layers of the organization. Step 4 is concerned with career path and keeping skills current and providing career path for the project managers and tracking their certifications and credentials. The training in an organization should address the various layers. Some of the types of training include:

- Executive level training where the executive of the organization learn through seminars and workshops about the PMO and how the project based management works Business unit managers level training were the managers collaborating with the PMO better understand the PMO and how project managers work and helps set the right expectations and increase synergies across all business units

- Project managers training and project team member training on process, methods, tools the organization adopt.
- Adhoc training includes one-on-one training for those requiring refreshers with central training repository to help individuals refer to at any time.

They are three parts to project managers' skills sustainability which would start in the set-up phase after an assessment of the skill set takes place to understand the type of skill training, on the job training, and career path growth.

The first part of an action plan allows projects managers to train at the basics level (organization methodology and process). By starting training all levels of managers with the core basics, project managers become grounded with the required methods and procedures that their organization considers critical for the successful delivery of a project. Specialized training for the various levels of project management is essential to expand their skills, develop their knowledge and keep them challenged for the next level of responsibility.

The second part of an action plan is to have a career path for the PMs to increase their competencies which will help ensure they progress to more senior project management roles, this crucial step can be achieved through working with Human Resources business unit and the PMO to set the career levels, performance criteria, etc for all project managers.

The third part of an action plan provide diversity in their assignments and work on projects that vary in size, type, and complexity, sharpening their skills across subject areas and business functions. This gives the PMO the opportunity to use the PM's experience and level to the fullest extent.

Step 5: Sustain executive commitments

This step is continuation of early stages building on executive support. The definition of executive role, and the governance authority should be defined in early stages. PMO executive sponsor should play an on-going active role in the PMO sustainability and contribute to providing inputs and direction to the PMO, taking away output and performance improvements to the realm of executives in the organization to show value and obtain commitment for PMO longevity. The key to help the PMO executive sponsor stand behind the PMO's mission relies on the PMO' showing continuous value add in the HR and customer value dimensions and minimizing the risks. Executives can identify with the power house of information provided by the PMO to enable their decisions and facilitate open discussions, the value has to be seen by all management layers within an organization. If the perception is that the PMO is adding value and enabling all layers of management within an organization, then the support and commitment will grow stronger. If on the other hand the PMO is perceived at any management layer as burden or adding more process work, the commitment will decline and it may lead at times to PMO failures

Step 6: Sustain continuous feedback loop

The continuous improvement journey starts with self-assessment and 360 assessment of the PMO. PMO needs to be transparent about annual goals and deliverables and improvement journey. PMO needs to enforce standards, quality, and measures; thus, it can be ranked and benchmarked based on it. PMO should institute soliciting feedback from executive management, other business unit functions, and project managers. PMO leaders need to build informal and formal channels for feedback.

Some of these formal channels are:

- Satisfaction survey that touches various levels within the organization
- Benchmark practices based on industry standards based on organization with similar industry practices
- Create PMO mailbox for Q&A and anonymous suggestions
- Publish goals and objectives and be transparent about the results and improvement plan.

Some of the informal channels are:

- Soliciting informal feedback from project managers, executives, functional managers
- Engaging project managers in soliciting feedback from their project team
- Meeting with the project sponsors to solicit performance feedback

Step 7: Sustain improvement action plan

All the above work should be confirmed in a PMO action plan (others may refer to it as execution plan), it is a documented PMO commitment to carry on with the continues improvement cycle defining the quality benchmark through continues feedback loop allows itemizing required improvement, set priority and approval as part of PMO sustainability plan.

Sustainability action plan should be a value based action plan were the focus is on bringing value internally and externally/ Acting on the defined interaction model and updating the interactions if required after consulting with organization executives.

Some large organizations have separate department of quality benchmark to ensure external audit to the PMO and allows the measure of sustainability efforts made by PMO against their set goals and objectives. Whether the approach is a self-audit or an audit by another entity, the audit criteria has to be built based on goals approved by organization executives and quality criteria and success criteria are set in early stages.

Some of the PMO value measure can be summarized in

- Metrics PMO collects and use of this metrics for decisions
- Methodologies and processes should be balanced to allow the right rigor for the right maturity stage
- Delivery improvement as a result of planning and governance structure
- Lesson learned effectiveness and how reflects in improving similar issues
- Improving transparency and collaboration at all levels of the organization

Existing PMO

Step 1: Re-align reporting performance

This step assumes that current reporting performance is not adequate, or can use improvement, or expectation has changed from Executives and the perception that the reports being generated to enable executives decision making need to be assessed and better lined up with the new expectation. PMO needs to revisit the current process in place and the content provided, as well as frequency of data distribution and make changes to either the process, the content, the frequency, or any combination.

From a process perspective, questions need to be asked are as follows:

- What types of reports need to be generated, or what existing reports need to be updated?
- Are the audience receiving these reports still the same, or has anything change?
- Does the frequency in sending these reports need to be updated?
- Is new reporting mechanism required (new tool, or new method to obtain data)?

From a content perspective, questions need to be asked are as follows:

- Has the data capture requirements changed?
- Is the presentation and layout of the data requiring updates?
- Is the current project data sufficient for enabling executives' decisions?

Reporting function is essential to organizations' ability to make right decisions at the right time. Focusing on the required flow of information and understanding organizations' requirements allows PMO to immediately remedy any reporting needs.

Step 2: Re-align support of PMO tools

To maintain the on-going support of PMO tools, PMO has to support issues, requests for project scheduling tools, project collaboration tools, and knowledge management tools; in addition, to improving tools usage and capabilities. This crucial step encompasses other steps:

- Stability and sustainability of current functions and ensure a measurement system that allows PMO to measure itself on the quality delivered, and ensure a strategy for improvements.

> This may entail a set of dashboards the reflect project progress, program progress, and portfolio progress.
> - Usability improving the ease of use of a tool, interaction of the tools, offering on-going support and minimizing user issues by addressing bottle necks and improving their interaction experience to ensure continuous improvement in scheduling, collaboration, and knowledge management sharing.

A Key to success lies in integrating current tools into a comprehensive delivery framework, and assessing the migration to other tools or expanding on current tools for improved performance. Some PMO's become center for various tools and usage becomes cumbersome that it may end up at times having adverse effect on the PMO in standardizing tools and compliance. Therefore, as a rule of thumb tools should automate good processes in place, and although at times tools are used as catalyst to enforce change, they need to be implemented with the right future process vision, they are never the answer for current broken process. Part of the on-going journey of existing PMOs is not to become tools heavy and leverage what's hot based on how the organization will maximize benefits of it. Example of nice mobile applications lately that connects teams and summarized their project tasks can be helpful tool for geographically disbursed teams and teams on the go, it may not have the same impact on teams that are collocated.

Step 3: Re-align training and mentoring programs

Step 4: Re-align PMO Staff skills and structure

These two steps speak to re-alignment of existing function, realignment assumes that a function has deviated from the set path, or gaps have been found in the current practices which require assessment and subsequently action plans to carry out the realignment activities. Action plans will vary in length and scope depending on the depth and breadth of the needed improvements, the organization's culture and structure and whether the projects managers are part of the PMO. For example, the type of training can enhance skills of project managers as well as provide general informational training in the organization to the non-project audience to heighten the awareness of project management and improve the understanding in general. Similarly, tools usage training is an important aspect of having a successful compliance using the tools and allowing users to maximize the benefit of the tools in use and understand the impact of efficient use. Training does not have to be big bang approach; it can be incremental and ongoing to ensure it touches all levels of the organization. Similarly all material pertaining to process, methodology, and tools need to be kept current with the evolving standards. There is a different type of training doesn't pertain to immediate need such as tools training or skills training, it contribute to the project managers career path. The category is education as in earning a degree to be a differentiator that could be industry base or a discipline base to allow project managers navigate through the ranks in the organization.

Learning through efforts to monitor performance against plan and learn from deviations, allow PMO to embed learning into action. Further understanding shifts in organization or external markets that demands shift in the organization; hence, adjustments to these skills would be required to ensure that PMO is not lagging behind and it is agile to take on adjustments and changes without disrupting PMO flow, or organization performance.

Step 5: Re-align executive commitments

This step is to renew the executive commitment that may have been lost due to many reasons. For example, PMO has not executed on the roadmap, or that PMO did not contribute to adding value in the HR or customer value dimension. At times the PMO may not seek to get direction, hence value-add may drop or perception of it have changed. On the other hand, executive support may not be as it used to which drives PMO to drop in value. Regardless of what caused the lack of commitment and support, the re-alignment and renovation of commitment is required and needs to be re-established on set objectives that can be measured and can be achieved.

Step 6: Re-establish continuous feedback loop

If for any reason, the PMO has stopped collecting feedback, or engaging all organization audience in the maturity stage, then an action is required to re-establish first a self-assessment, then executive assessment which ensures executive commitment as in the previous step, then allowing the project managers to reflect and provide feedback on the use of the templates, tools, processes. To re-establish the feedback can happen through various mechanism, survey were anonymous feedback is collected, one-on-one interviews with executives and general perception of whether the PMO is implementing on the feedback.

Step 7: Re-establish improvement action plan

Re-establishing the improvement action plan means looking at the previous action plan and assessing what is still valid, what needs to change, or taken out. The reason the improvement plan may need to be re-established is that some plans are monitored and controlled to ensure adoption and continuous improvements are being executed; hence, the improvement may not take place as planned. The plan should be value base action plans were the focus is on bringing value to the HR and customer dimensions.

Sustainability toolkit

Whether you are setting up a new PMO or reestablishing an existing function, it is vital that you establish a means to demonstrate (a) the value of the PMO consistently and appropriately and (b) the flexibility and adaptability of the PMO in the face of ongoing business change.

There are four elements have been defined that will ensure PMO's sustainability journey is successful.

PMO Communication

A well balanced communication starts with transparency. That involves defining a process to handle what information is communicated, the media that are used, the frequency of the information flow, and who the audience is who are receiving the information. Communicating project progress, portfolio progress, or PMO sustainability progress are important and discrete elements of any communication plan. For example, this may include summary reports describing KPI representing project, program, and portfolio health check. In other reports, it might be detailed financial analysis, or various representation of resource allocation broken by project, by department, and by title. Consideration to the planning media is important to determine how much information may be delivered by a 'push' medium (a newsletter, an ex-mail, a blog or a report) and how much may be delivered to self-service platforms such as intranets, or 'pull' medium (BI tools that allow users real time data analysis). Training the PMO audience on how to use these reports and perform analysis will allow these audiences to become more educated with KPI and measures, and improve their reporting requests as a result decisions will be improved.

PMO Governance

It is expected that a PMO build a governance model, improve existing governance, and enforces the required gates to ensure compliance. Well-structured governance will include the various levels of functions and define their roles, their responsibilities, and what decisions are they able to make. Governance ensures that the overall corporate standardization and performance assessment and measurements are consistent. Below in figure 4.4 is an example that shows organization structure that embeds governance based on the organization hierarchy. While PMO reports into the CEO in this example, it is at the same level as other business units in the organization. The project team at the work stream level is comprised from the functions that report into these business units. It is important to define the governance model based on organization culture and depending on where the PMO reports into. Furthermore, the governance structure should be visited as part of annual refinement and re-alignment if needed.

Figure 4.4 Sample organization structure model

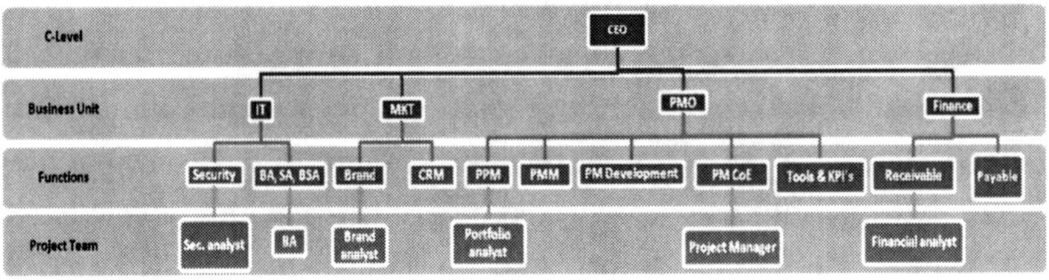

PMO Knowledge Repository

Regardless of what type of PMO an organization has adopted whether it is consulting, authoritarian, or knowledge, it has the potential to become a power house of information, a business intelligence mechanism that takes all types of project data (resource efforts, budget, time, deliverables, etc) and turn it into valuable information that can be used at the various management levels of an organization. For team members provide them with repository of available training, certification requirements and availability, lesson learned database from all projects to share and learn from, case studies, and industry links to up to date information that can be used for professional progress and job improvement. For business units managers, provide them with resource information to allow them improving resource planning and forecasting, and lessons learned from their resources which will help resource managers allocate the matching skill for the type of project. For executives, implement reporting capabilities, and improve existing to improve analytics, dashboard reporting to enable decision making. For PMO leaders, availability of data and tools to present the information at all levels and allow PMO leaders to enhance the performance measure which is one of the greatest benefits in building the knowledge repository.

PMO Performance

A reason for creating a PMO is to guarantee consistency of approach across projects. As organization seek more efficiencies and increased performance from projects, they turned to establishing project management offices (PMO) to instill the needed discipline of PM (Santosus, 2003). PMO is a function within an organization that provides project management service to support an organization's projects delivery and contribute to the performance of the organization through standardized processes and practices.

Performance can be defined as the success in achieving pre-defined goals and objective for an organization to achieve financial and non-financial rewards. Performance management is branch of performance that focuses on performance of the organization, a department, or processes to build a product or services, employees, etc (Paladino, 2007). The essence of performance is creating value for an organization producing goods and/or services, so that it stays in existence for the organization's clients. Hofer, 2006 and Porter, 1985 describe the important functions for performance to be value creation and competitive advantage.

Value creation as we have explored in the previous chapter is through customer value and resource value allowing the organization to produce quality products and services for its customers, and allow the organization to motivate and improve people performance.

PMO Challenges

As there are four elements to ensure PMO's sustainability journey is successful. There are four Major challenges for a PMO and these could impede the sustainability journey if not given careful consideration.

Process & Methodology

While it is great to have processes and agreed upon standard methodology in place, it is very counterproductive when processes become the center of the work and for the sake of processes and do not serve the organization as a whole. For example, following the same rigor of procedures or protocols, templates and guidelines without consideration to the efforts involved and the size of project will make PMO be perceived as an over-kill, and soon the PMO will lose credibility among both project managers and the organization's leadership team. To overcome this challenge, PMO need to be starting small and focusing on the pain areas is much more effective than building everything at once and then tripping in the rollout due to the level of the maturity of the organization. Unless the organization from the PM's up to the leadership team is ready to take on a large magnitude of change. Please remember first and foremost, the reason for methodology and processes are to allow for improvements in both effectiveness and efficiency, not to create bureaucracy for project managers and the organization as a whole.

Project Managers Skill Level

Another challenge for PMO is failure to assess the project managers' skill sets correctly. The PMO head will be caught by surprise when ready to roll-out the processes and/ or methodologies to be faced with a huge gap between a PM's skill set and their knowledge of the methodology, tools, etc. The gap in the skill set may delay or prolong methodology rollout and/or adoption. Some of these gaps might be due to a previous practice that is not necessarily wrong but doesn't work with that particular organization, or sometimes simply this is a new position for someone, or someone who ran projects like a maverick and does not understand why they need to comply with the new rules. To overcome this challenge, the work of creating methodology and assessing and educating PM's needs to happen in parallel and in unison. While creating methodology, there should be assessment to the levels of maturity and skills level of an organizations project managers, whether they are existing PM's or any new PM or promoted PM to determine the education required to bring all to if not the same level, to a very close level so that performance measurements can be close.

Project and Portfolio Tools

In any new function implementation, it is the function people, then process, and finally tools that make PMO and any other function efficient. Implementing any tool before having the earlier two (people and process) would be a recipe for failure. Even if the processes are simple and the methodology is not completely polished, there should be a process in place that govern the use of the tool and how people will use it and identifying the outcome the PMO is trying to achieve. Any new PMO should be careful from imposing a project and/ or a portfolio tools set before having people ready and well trained and the processes have been established. The tools are now far more sophisticated and not only serve the PM, but are a complete platform of applications that will allow for project building, tracking, budget monitoring, document collaboration, analytics and reporting, etc. All goes back to understanding the organization's requirements and what is required out of the tool; relying on a 3rd party to tell the PMO what they would get out of a tool is fatal. Being educated and understanding the organization's requirements when approaching a project or portfolio tool and treating it as you would treat deploying any organizational system such as CRM, ERP, etc is critical.

Establish Best Practices

With newly formed PMOs, best practices are often neglected either due to the unavailability of man power that can be dedicated for that purpose, or because the PMO is working on the next level of expansion and not taking the time to measure and assess the current state before proceeding with any improvements. PMO should start gathering best practices data whether documenting lesson learned, methodology improvement, effective tools usage, etc. Retaining all of the best practices work in a centralized place that is easy to access is very important. Also, it is important to regularly communicate the updates and changes so that everyone stays up-to-date with the changes, and that it becomes the library of best practices for the benefit of all levels of an organization.

The graph at the end of this chapter depicts the overall PMO sustainability phase, along with the seven step process

Chapter Summary

In this chapter, the reader has been presented with the PMO sustainability steps. The seven steps to sustain a newly built PMO or existing PMO. The chapter further discusses sustainability principles and definitions; the human resource value-add and customer value-add. The chapter concluded with the sustainability toolkit which is comprised of four elements and these are PMO communication, PMO governance, PMO knowledge repository, and PMO performance.

CHAPTER 5

PMO Survey Results

PMOs have been taking on a more prominent role in their level of authority, structure, reporting lines and mandate. Project Management Offices (PMOs) have been growing and going through change and transformation and today literature defines PMO types, roles, functions, as well as their impact on performance. The lifecycle journey that PMOs go through requires attention since there is little or lack of knowledge regarding the PMO lifecycle (PMOLC) pertaining to set-up, build-out, and sustainability.

Due to the evolution of the PMO and there is a need to cover the lifecycle of PMO which would allow those interested in building PMOs to learn what is required in each phase of the PMOLC, the complexities associated with each phase, the challenges and the rewards. The PMOLC has not been fully explored nor has it been discussed in detail; hence, this research makes valuable contributions to the practicality of the project management field in general, and sheds light on the PMO practices in particular. Further, the research adds valuable insights to the mechanics governing the establishment of PMOs. Results will lead us to:

- Determine the PMOLC complexities, shed light on the nature of each phase, and the skills required to build each phase
- Determine similar and different challenges in each phase in the lifecycle

Survey Set-up

A survey was conducted to collect data regarding the set-up, build-out, and sustainability of the PMO. The survey was a web-based survey uses 5-point Likert-type scale and was developed and made available on-line for PMO leaders who set-up, or built, or supported a PMO, these were PMO professional volunteers across geography and industries. There were 100 respondents to the survey, 67 have completed it.

Research results from the web-based survey lead to the finding that PMO set-up and build-out phases are more complex than the sustainability phase. Additionally, the findings show the effect of executive leadership support in an organization and the skill set and role of the PMO leader.

Survey Sections

The survey instrument was divided into three sections. Before any sections, an introduction section was provided that stated the purpose of the study, set expectations, and provided guidance and the deadline to complete the survey (Appendix C).

Section one
PMO set-up, build-out, and sustainability questions ranged from question 1-12. This section surveyed type of PMO, where PMO reported into, type of executive level PMO reported into, skills it takes to set-up a PMO, build-out a PMO, and sustain the PMO.

Section two
PMO organizational questions ranged from questions 13-21. This section surveyed PMO change management, PMO leadership support, and project managers' reporting structure PMOs

Section three
General categorical and demographic information (such as gender, age, geographic location, etc)

Because survey takers were required to conform to criteria (Cooper & Schindler, 2003) by not only possessing the specific knowledge of PMO required, also leading or have lead PMO set-up, or build-out, or support PMO initiative to be eligible to answer the survey questions (Biemer et al., 1991), a sampling frame (Simon & Burstein, 1969) was created. The sampling frame was necessary because randomly selecting elements from the total population of project management PMO professionals to solicit judgments from experienced PMO leaders. Preferably, according to Wright and Tsao (1983), the determination of a sampling frame should consider the following: objectives of the survey, population of interest, data to be collected, etc.

With these considerations, the author identified and made up the sampling frame which consists of the following: PMOForum, PMI CoP, PMO leads through professional network (Europe, Canada, US, Asia, other).

A simple convenience sample was taken from the sampling frame, allowing each subject an equal chance of responding to the survey and being included in the sample (Simon & Burstein, 1969). Each group within the sampling frame was solicited on from March 2011 through June 2011. A web based tool was used to collect responses and store data (Sekaran, 2003). The sampling frame made a total of 100 respondents logged on to the survey website from April 2011 - June 2011. Not all respondents who started the survey completed it, eight were excluded because they have not completed first question. All remaining respondents who partially completed the survey stopped at the start of new section. Of the 92 who took the survey, 67 completed the survey for a completion rate of 73%.

The survey was designed using closed questions (Wheater & Cook, 2000). Survey questions for categorical items. Survey questions for continuous variables were created using 5-point Likert-type scale (Likert, 1967; Miller, 1983). Each question began by presenting an affirmative declaration of the variable items followed by a 5-point Likert-type anchored on the far left end with Strongly Disagree or not important and on the far right with Strongly Agree or most important (see Appendix D). N/A was included at the far right of the scale.

This survey analysis consists of 2 sections. Section 1 provides the descriptive statistics of categorical variable data, while Section 2 provides descriptive analysis of continuous variable data.

Analysis of Categorical Data

Categorical Data

The survey instrument collected categorical information for descriptive purposes. The following categorical data was collected: geographic location, age group, and gender.

Respondents came from various geographical locations. The largest number of respondents was from Canada at 35%, followed by the 25% from the US. Table 5.1 show % of these respondents.

Geographic Location	Percentage	Frequency
US,	25%	14
Canada,	35%	19
Latin America	4%	2
Europe,	20%	11

Australia		0%	0
Asia Pacific		4%	2
Other, please specify:		13%	7
TOTAL		100%	55

The largest number of respondents, 45%, belonged to the 35-44 age groups. The second largest age group, 35%, belonged to the 45-54 age groups. Results are shown in table 5.2

Age		Percentage	Frequency
Under 25		0%	0
25-34		4%	2
35-44		45%	25
45-54		35%	19
55-64		16%	9
65 or Above		0%	0
TOTAL		100%	55

The largest number of respondents, 62%, was male, while 38% were female. Results in graph 5.1 below

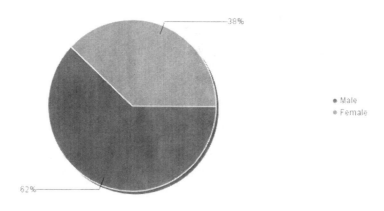

Descriptive Analysis of Continuous Data

The following section provides descriptive statistics of continuous survey data. The statistics were derived from Likert-type scale responses.

How many PMOs does your organization have? The highest number is 63% for the Category "only one PMO", followed by 28% for the Category "more than 3 PMO's". Table 5.3 show the details to the question

Number of PMOs	Percentage	Frequency
1 PMO only	63%	42
2-3 PMOs	9%	6
More than 3 PMOs	28%	19
TOTAL	100%	67

Where does your PMO reside? The highest rating of 40% was for PMO's residing at the corporate level, followed by 31% residing in IT. Table 5.4 show the details to the question

PMO Resides in	Percentage	Frequency
Independent organization (outsourced or virtual PMO)	6%	4
Corporate level	40%	27
IT	31%	21
Other, please specify:	22%	15
TOTAL	100%	67

Where does your PMO report into? The highest rating was 24% for PMO's reporting into C level in an organization, followed by 22% of PMO's reporting into CIO. Table 5.5 show the details to the question

PMO Reporting line	Percentage	Frequency
CEO	15%	10
CFO	4%	3
CIO	22%	15
C level executive under CEO	24%	16
Executive under C Level business side	15%	10
Executive under C level IT side	7%	5
Other, please specify:	12%	8
TOTAL	100%	67

What level of management leads your PMO? The highest rating was 34% for PMO leaders at the Executive level, followed by 31% as Directors. Table 5.6 show the details to the question

Management Level	Percentage	Frequency
C-Level	13%	9
Executive (Someone who reports into a C-level)	33%	22
Director	31%	21

Manager		16%	11
Consultant		4%	3
Other, please specify:		1%	1
TOTAL	100%		67

How do you define your PMO authority/influence in the company's hierarchy? The highest rating was 49% for PMO authority through executive, followed by 25% for PMO being involved at the C level discussions. Table 5.7 show the details to the question

PMO's Authority	Percentage	Frequency
PMO is involved at the highest boards C level discussion	25%	17
PMO is involved through an executive at C level discussions	49%	33
PMO is only involved at business unit level (departmental)	22%	15
Other, please specify:	3%	2
TOTAL	**100%**	**67**

The skills of a PMO head to build a PMO may differ from those to run a PMO. The highest rating was 36% were survey participants believe that the PMO lead skill set do differ between phases (set-up & build-out) vs. sustainability, followed by 24% of extreme opposite were PMO lead skill as seen would not differ regardless of PMOLC phase. Table 5.8 show the details to the question

PMO Leaders Skills	Percentage	Frequency
PMO in-charge skill set differ only between (set-up, build-out) vs. sustainability	36%	21
PMO in-charge skill set differ only between set-up vs. (build-out, sustainability)	17%	10
PMO in-charge skill set differ only between (set-up vs. build-out vs. sustainability	14%	8
PMO in-charge skill set do not differ regardless of a phase	24%	14
PMO in-charge skill set do differ regardless of a phase	10%	6
TOTAL	**100%**	**59**

What is your role in the PMO set-up and build-out? The highest rating was 52% for those who built a none existing PMO. Table 5.9 show the details to the question

Role in PMO Setup & Build-out	Percentage	Frequency
I built a none-existing PMO	52%	35
I re-built an existing PMO	19%	13

	Percentage	Frequency
Other, please specify:	0%	0
I was contracted to build the PMO only	9%	6
Other, please specify:	19%	13
TOTAL	100%	67

What is your role in the PMO sustainability and support? The highest rating was 64% for those who support the PMO they built. Table 5.10 show the details to the question

Role in PMO Sustainability	Percentage	Frequency
I support the PMO I built	64%	43
I support an already built PMO	19%	13
I was contracted to support a built PMO only	4%	3
Other, please specify:	12%	8
TOTAL	100%	67

Rank the complexity in the PMO lifecycle phases (set-up, build-out, sustainability) The highest rating was 44% for PMOLC being complex in setup-and build-out, opposed to 17% viewed it as most complex. Table 5.11 show the details to the question

Managing The PMO Lifecycle

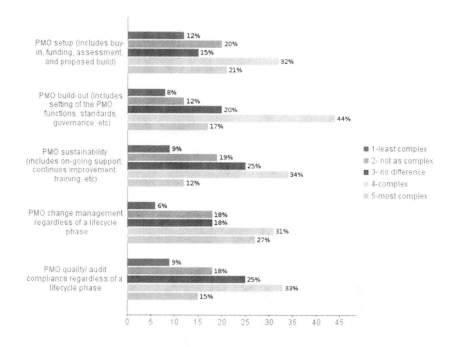

What type of Authority does your PMO have? The highest rating was 56% for compliance/ authoritative PMO type. Graph 5.2 show the details to the question

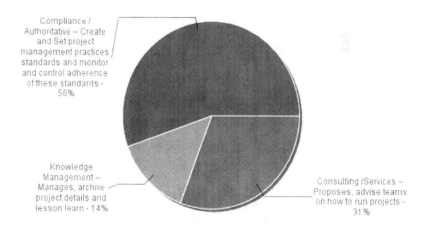

What are the unique challenges in the Setup and build-out phase? The highest rating was 71% for buy-in, followed by 69% for leadership support. Table 5.12 show the details to the question

Challenges in set-up & Build-out	Percentage	Frequency
Funding	29%	17
Buy-in	71%	42
Leadership support	69%	41
Cost / Value	29%	17
Business case	29%	17
Skill set	27%	16
Governance	42%	25
Methodology adoption	34%	20
Other, please specify:	2%	1
TOTAL	100%	59

What are the unique challenges in the sustainability phase? The highest rating was 66% for continues improvements, followed by 65% Reports/KPI. Table 5.13 show the details to the question

Challenges in Sustainability	Percentage	Frequency
Continuous improvement	66%	39
Reports / KPI	56%	33

	Percentage	Frequency
Quality management / measurement	53%	31
Cost / Value	32%	19
Standards	29%	17
Project performance	53%	31
Project recovery	14%	8
Tools adoption	36%	21
Other, please specify:	7%	4
TOTAL	100%	59

In my organization, I can describe the level of executive buy-in as. The highest rating was 42% for medium executive support. Table 5.14 show the details to the question

Executive buy-in	Percentage	Frequency
100% Executive support—High	34%	20
80% Executive support—Medium	42%	25
50% Executive support—Low	17%	10
Less than 50% Executive support—very low	7%	4
TOTAL	100%	59

Do you believe change management and project management adoption in an organization is correlated to the level of PMO's authority? The highest rating was 76% for "The higher the authority, the more PMO's influence in change mgmt and PM". Table 5.15 show the details to the question

Change Mgmt & PM Adoption	Percentage	Frequency
The higher the authority, the more PMO's influence in change mgmt and PM adoption	76%	45
The lower the authority, the less PMO's influence in change mgmt and PM adoption	7%	4
The level of authority doesn't impact PMO's influence in change mgmt and PM adoption	15%	9
Other, please specify:	2%	1
TOTAL	**100%**	**59**

Does your PMO have responsibility for delivery of projects? 68% of the PMOs have responsibility for delivery of projects. Graph 5.3 show the details to the question

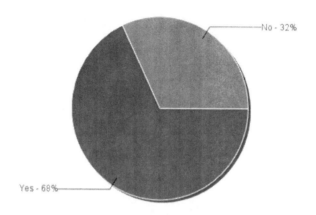

How many Projects does your PMO manage in a year? The highest rating was 34% for managing 1-20 projects. Table 5.16 show the details to the question

PMO Managed Projects	Percentage	Frequency
1-20 Projects	34%	20
21-50 Projects	28%	16
51-100 Projects	19%	11
More than 100 Projects	19%	11
TOTAL	**100%**	**58**

Please select one of the maturity levels below that best describes your PMO? The highest rating was 31% for "level 3—Defined level. Table 5.17 show the details to the question

PMO Maturity Level	Percentage	Frequency
Initial Level—ad hoc and chaotic; relies on the competence of individuals and no standards in place	19%	11
Repeatable Level—System and structure is in place based on previous experience.	29%	17
Defined Level—Standard system and structure organization wide of performed activities	31%	18
Managed Level—Established and measured processes against organizational goals; deviations are identified and managed.	19%	11
Optimizing Level—the entire organization is focused on continuous improvement	3%	2
TOTAL	100%	59

Managing The PMO Lifecycle

What functions does your PMO perform today? The highest rating was 80% for project/ program governance, followed by 71% methodology management. Table 5.18 show the details to the question

PMO Functions Performed	Percentage	Frequency
Portfolio management	62%	34
Methodology management	71%	39
Tools implementation	64%	35
Project/ program governance	80%	44
Project/ program standards	71%	39
Project manager training	62%	34
Resource capacity planning	45%	25
KPI and Reporting	64%	35
Project/ program assessment and quality check	58%	32
Other, please specify:	5%	3
TOTAL	**100%**	**55**

What benefits does your Executive get today out of your PMO? The highest rating was 70% for consistent project method and delivery, followed by 69% for improved project governance and change control. Table 5.19 show the details to the question

PMO's Benefits to Executives	Percentage	Frequency
Improved Project Standardization	67%	36
Improved standardization of Operation	33%	18
Unified decision making across the Enterprise	41%	22
Faster access to quality information	50%	27
Better capacity planning (resource planning)	46%	25
Consistent project method of delivery	70%	38
Improved project governance and change control	69%	37
Improved project performance	52%	28
TOTAL	100%	54

What are the challenges that your PMO faces today? The highest rating was 63% for project management maturity, followed by 59% portfolio management alignment. Table 5.20 show the details to the question

PMO Challenges	Percentage	Frequency
Project management maturity,	63%	34
Portfolio management alignment	59%	32
Adoption of methodologies	37%	20
Adoption of tools,	37%	20
Leadership support,	33%	18
Lack of project managers kill set,	39%	21
Cost control,	28%	15
Other, please specify:	17%	9
TOTAL	**100%**	**54**

In your organizations, project managers report into: The highest rating was 35% for reporting into the business units, followed by 30% for Reporting into the PMO only. Table 5.21 show the details to the question

Project Managers Report into	Percentage	Frequency
PMO only	30%	16
Business Units only (IT included as a business unit)	35%	19
50% PMO, 50% Business unit	17%	9
20% PMO, 80% Business unit	13%	7
80% PMO, 20% Business unit	6%	3
TOTAL	100%	54

Discussion

The survey's objective was to investigate the PMOLC and find out the phases in the lifecycle and able to provide information that aid PMO leads, executives, and those internal to a PMO or external to be able to maximize advantages and minimize disadvantages. Some of the questions that were seeking to address are:

- Which phase in the PMO lifecycle is more complex?
- What are PMO challenges in each phase in the lifecycle?
- What is the PMO leader's role in PMO lifecycle?
- How does the level of PMO authority impact change management and project management?

Research results from the web-based survey lead to the finding that PMO set-up and build-out phases are more complex than sustainability phase. Additionally, the findings show the effect of executives leadership support in an organization and the skill set and role of the PMO leader.

Summary of Survey Finding

Survey outcome lead to the conclusion that PMOLC is complex; the set-up and build-out phases are more complex than sustainability phase. Additionally, the findings show the effect of executives leadership support in an organization and the skill set and role of the PMO leader in the various phases; as well as the level of authority of PMO and its impact on project management and change management in an organization.

The overall result show that PMO continues to evolve and take a prominent role in the organization hierarchy as seen in the survey majority of PMO leaders are at the C level or reporting to C level, PMO reporting into executive office and that 34% of surveyed reported that projects are managed through their PMO.

➢ PMOLC complexity
 The findings of this research describe the complexity of PMOLC. Whether one or more of the three PMOLC phases (set-up, build-out, and sustainability) are more or less complex than the other. The survey suggests that 44% found the build-out most complex, while 34% found sustainability to be the most complex, followed by 32% for the set-up.

➢ PMOLC challenges
 The findings of this research describe the challenges of PMOLC and identify similarities or differences based on each phase. While funding, leadership support, and governance were ranked high as

challenges pertaining to set-up and build-out phase, the survey found continuous improvement, reporting/KPI, and quality management to be the highest on list of challenges pertaining to the sustainability phase. While cost / value ranked closely as a challenge for all phases ranging between 29% and 32%, similarly the adoption of methods or tools ranked at the same level independent of the PMOLC phase ranging between 34% to 36%.

> PMO leaders leadership skills
>
> The findings of this research describe the various skill set and leadership qualities required to run the various PMOLC phases. While 36% believe that the skill set and leadership required to run (set-up and build-out) are different from those of the sustainability phase, 24% believe that the leadership and skill set do not differ regardless of PMOLC phase.

In addition, the survey shows the role of individuals in the PMOLC phase and whether those who set-up and build-out, do sustain the PMO or each phase is independent of who did it. When PMO leaders were asked about their role in each phase of the PMOLC, 52% had built a non-existent PMO, while 19% re-built or transformed an existing PMO and these results pertain to the PMOLC phases of set-up and build-out.

> PMO Authority and adoption
>
> The findings of this research describe the level of authority of PMO and its impact on project management and change management adoption in an organization. The results show a strong correlation between the levels of authority PMO has and the level of change management and project management adoption. The survey shows that 76% believe that the higher the authority, the more PMO's influence in change management and PM adoption.

In another question surveying the types of PMO's authority, 56% of PMOs were authoritative. The overall results show more PMO's are adopting authoritarian role which is having an impact on increased adoption in change management and project management.

Lastly, the survey shows that the reporting level of PMO and PMO leaders' title and position in the organization is on the rise. 40% of PMOs reside at corporate level, and 47% of PMO leaders at the C or Executive level.

Chapter Summary

In this chapter, the reader has been presented the results of PMO survey that highlighted the complexity of the PMOLC, and shed light on the nature of each phase, and the skills required to build each phase. Further illustrate similar and different challenges in each phase in the lifecycle

CHAPTER 6

PMO CONTROVERSIAL TRENDS

It is quite common to have controversies within each discipline, project management and PMO no different from other discipline. There are many controversies still surrounding project management, the author will focus on the following areas: in-sourcing and out-sourcing, PMO as a temporary organization or a permanent one, PPM within PMO or managed separately, project management precedes PMO or PMO is catalyst to building project management. The author's objective in the new section is to shed light and provide insights to the different schools of thoughts surrounding each of these areas allowing the reader to benefit from various thinking and incorporate what fits their culture, structure, and future vision. Chapter eight will present case studies presenting each organization practices and how they have dealt with these areas to ensure the success of their set-up, build-out, and sustainability.

PMO or Project Management

Did PMO or Project management come first; it is like the chicken and the egg question. Project management is a discipline that existed for the longest time; therefore, from that perspective project management as a practice came before the notion of project management office. Although the numbers of PMOs in organizations are on the rise, there are organizations that have the project management discipline and they exercise a level of governance without having a PMO or other names for a central function running project management. One size does not fit all; hence, organizations should look to what is feasible for them and not to build PMO because other organizations are building PMOs. There will always be some level of project management practiced within organization formal or informal. Whether organization acknowledge the practice and formalize a function that nurture it, or run it adhoc that is dependent on organization culture, resources, nature of their business, and manner in which they go about delivering their products or services.

Today, some organizations believe that an organization should have some level of project management even if it is basic before having a PMO. The requirements of practicing project management need to be in place before a PMO exist. There are those of the view that PMO should be come first, then the organization build project management discipline in an organization.

Advantages to having PMO first might be that project management will be done based on best practices, further, it will be based on industry standards such as PMI to ensure availability of templates, processes, and tools. Advantages to having project management first is the knowledge that project management is needed and being practiced; hence the function PMO to be created can have a definite mandate on what is being practiced and what's being achieved.

The author's objective is to stir the thinking and allow organizations and individuals involved to take the opportunity to evaluate the possibilities in which will be further highlighted and elaborated in chapter seven on how actually organizations dealt with project management and PMO

Some questions organizations need to ask on having PMO vs. project management are:

- How mature is the project management practice within the organization
- How does the organization organize their portfolio planning
- Does each department run their own projects or is there a mandate to have standard method of delivery

The answers to these questions should be taken in consideration, would an organization invest in a finance department prior to having finances being run in an organization, or should there be a financial practice and then an organization formalize the practices into a finance department. This example touches on scale, budget, and the need to have an informal practice vs. formalized function.

Temporary or Permanent

It is very important when looking into organizations requirement of the desired PMO to understand the mandate and objectives of having a PMO. The decision of PMO becoming temporary function or permanent function depends on organization's culture, structure, and future vision. While some would think the smaller an organization, the more temporary a PMO could be, and that large companies have the infrastructure to invest in a permanent PMO. All these theories will depend on organization culture, their ability to adopt project based processes and adapt to changes, their structure starting from organization structure to governance dynamics, to the process of making decisions. Future vision is important; whether PMO is a core function in an organization or in-time function to deliver specific objective.

Despite the number of PMO's that are on the rise, the view of whether this organism PMO is a temporary endeavor similar to a project or is it a permanent function seems to be still a debate among practitioners and of course theorist who ultimately base their studies based on the realities of organizations.

<u>Make it temporary.</u> Those who support this notion rely heavily on that project management is about temporary organization, the definition of project that it is temporary endeavor as PMBOK suggests, and then it must be that the organization governing projects be temporary dissolves as projects dissolve. That organization project management should grow organically and when it does, some discipline concentrated in a function can help move project management adoption. Once that is established the function does not need to exist and the practice can be carried along and adopted.

<u>Make it permanent.</u> Those who support this notion rely on the fact that to run continuous projects and to support standards, and project managers, you need the support of an organization that provide guideline and measure for following standards, or how else the project practice will evolve and improve. When the objective for a PMO is to become a CoE to oversee the delivery, project managers training and career path, then it might not be feasible to have a core function as a temporary function

What is misleading in some literature is the timing of some PMO's being considered temporary by that PMO's have a life span shorter than three years. There are projects that run over three years in many industries, certainly in the pharmaceutical industry and hence, the PMO that existed to support these projects would last as long as the project lasts. There are various reasons of why organization implement PMOs, one of the main is managed cross-functional; hence, the numbers of PMOs are on the rise, not on the decline. Others argue that PMO transform and hence they are not stable or temporary in nature. Many other functions have seen transformations and do see transformation every day between centralizing functions, decentralizing function, re-vitalization in terms of roles and responsibilities, all these part of the evolution of functions and dynamics of organization and less of reflection on a particular department or a function within an organization

PMO's originated around supporting the one project organization and as organization progressed in project managing adoption and the discipline of managing by project "projectized" became the way of delivery through managing multi-projects. The issue of PMO's being shutdown or transformed is not any different from the larger organization transformation initiative. Organizations may eliminate the title of a function and have it under another but certainly some of the tasks remain carried out by a new function or combined with other functions. There are pros and cons to having a PMO for an organization; however, the statistics and most recent done on the state of the PMO shows that PMO is on the rise with 84% of organizations have PMOs and these PMOs are strategic partners (pmsolutions, 2010)

The reader should distinguish between the temporary natures of some PMOs and the value-add that a PMO may or may not provide. A PMO can be temporarily created to run a massive organization project and bring a value-add either in the customer value, and HR value. While a long term PMO may do the opposite and misses on adding value.

Some questions organizations need to ask regarding the PMOs state are:

- What are the reasons and drivers for establishing a PMO
- What are the short term vs. long term benefits
- Is the PMO tactical in nature or strategic partner
- Is funding available to support the creation and sustainability of PMO

- Dies the PMO have the required executive support
- How to define success and how to measure it to determine if a PMO is doing a "good" job.

Depends on the answers to the questions above, an organization can determine the permanent or temporary nature of a PMO.

Insource or Outsource

It is very important when looking at outsourcing and insourcing decisions to consider the culture, structure, and future vision. While some would think the smaller an organization, the better it would benefit from outsourcing a PMO and that large companies have the infrastructure to have their internal PMO. All these theories will depend on organization culture, their ability to adopt project based processes and adapt to changes, their structure starting from organization structure to governance dynamics, to the process of making decisions. Future vision is important; it is not about building a PMO today and not being able to sustain it, or outsource it and find that wasn't the best way to get benefits from PMO. Insourcing and outsourcing decisions has been made in other functions such as IT, call centers, etc. It should not be an unfamiliar phenomenon and organizations should take advantage when it complements their culture, structure, and future vision.

Outsourcing is the act of obtaining services from an external source (Brown and Wilson, 2005, p 20). Organizations and individuals have been outsourcing for long time without knowing it. Outsourcing is not only sending jobs off-shore as some believe, although that what brought the highlight into outsourcing practice. A job/task can be performed by internal resources of an organization or external to the organization. Outsourcing in particular became popular in recent years due to globalizations and companies involved in various markets seeking to maximize profit and minimize cost which is one of the main drivers to outsourcing. Other drivers to outsourcing have been access to specialized skill sets and large number of them in a particular period of time, improve speed of delivery, focus internal employees on core tasks which meant only non-core functions have been outsourced. Although that depends between an organization and another on what is considered core functions/tasks. In general, core tasks have to do with company's intellectual property, core business drivers that impact their clients and their competitive edge in their market.

What functions have been outsourced? Outsourcing started in manufacturing mainly for cost reduction and then the trend moved into other important organizational functions such as finance, payroll, tax, HR, call centers, and services. (Brown and Wilson, 2005)

Some of the advantages outsourcing, it provided smaller organization to have similar skills and reduced cost to allow them stay competitive. Outsourcing allowed organizations to focus on core strategic initiatives. Some of the disadvantages to outsourcing is loss of jobs at times, and further impact to deliverable quality. Another disadvantage is potentially jeopardizing security in handling intellectual property.

The question of whether to outsource or insource is not an easy one and only organization can assess to outsource, to insource, to go hybrid and outsource some functions and keep others. The key to understanding the balance and trade-offs lie in organization understanding to their vision, direction, and their own definition of success.

Some of the questions organizations need to ask regarding outsourcing PMO are:

- What areas of PMO to outsource
- What are the Pros and cons to outsourcing PMO
- When outsourcing make sense and when it doesn't

- How to maximize the benefit of outsourcing model
- What are the selection criteria for the outsourcing partner?

As outsourcing has been popular for non-core activities to allow organizations PMO to focus on core activities and to better support the needs of the organization and drive the expected value-add. Outsourcing tool sets, application, and project platforms can be beneficial to outsource if an organization ability to maintain projects tools might be more cumbersome and more expensive to perform than allowing SME to host the application. At the same time SME hosting the application have to provide companies with services and support that will assure the agent organization the appropriate service level which again needs to be documented in Service level agreements (SLA).

Another PMO function has been outsourced, project managers and training. When project managers are contracted this is a form of outsourcing, this does not suggest that every organization contract project managers. Most organizations use hybrid model was they have full time project managers and augment these project managers with outsourced project managers. Similarly training has been outsourced to companies that can train on project management topics including certifications and accreditation.

Other companies have outsourced different functions as well, all dependent again on where would a company maximize their benefit, improve cost, and focus on core functions.

PPM or PMO

Having portfolio management is a sign of organizational recognition of linking strategy with execution. Some organizations link strategy and execution under one function, while others separate them into two functions, one that's concerned with Strategy and the other with execution. When organizations decide their structure, they should look at keeping groups close, yet, ensuring there is no conflict of interest amongst these groups.

For some organization, having PMO and PPM together is optimal because of the close collaboration that is required between team members. Those organizations that choose to combine strategy and execution under one function represented in the PMO tend to be in general smaller organization in size, smaller portfolio size, and budget. PMOs were established to coordinate portfolios of projects from executive boards and facilitate selection, monitoring and controlling projects. (Andersen et al., 2007). In these organizations linking strategy and execution is tightly coupled and maybe the head of the PMO running both functions.

While the organizations that have chosen to separate PPM from PMO, the focus might be different and for mainly strategic reasons such as size of PPM, the focus required for PPM and PMO, and the organization structures. In these organizations, the PPM size is multimillion dollar that spans various organizational division across geography. In that case the PPM requires a dedication to be run to achieve focus on strategy. Further, in these organizations, PMO is focused on project delivery, the execution of the approved and prioritized portfolio, while PPM is focused on portfolio management through the annual planning cycle; which in many organizations is linked to the fiscal year planning, budget planning, and strategic roadmap plans. The hand over from PPM to PMO and vice versa is crucial to ensure resources and efforts are focused on the right initiatives.

Reference to an organization that separated PPM from PMO is in chapter seven, page 159. In this organization, The PPM head is involved throughout the PMO lifecycle to understand the value of an initiative and determine if an initiative needs to stop and another starts and advice the PMO with that, while the PMO head focus is on delivering the assigned initiative per the priority sequence provided by the PPM process. The separation in duty, yet the collaboration across PMO and PPM was synchronized through a governance model that details who, how, when, and the gates involved between PMO and PPM to allow the continuous flow of information and timeliness of this information. The need for continuous dialogue between the two functions is critical to ensure synergy and optimization of individual project delivery and overall Portfolio benefit realization.

Those organizations that choose to separate strategy from execution have done it based on having large number of initiatives, multi million dollars budget, complexity in organization structure, and scope of work. Generally these organizations have hundreds of projects with multi million dollars budget crossing an enterprise or even global capacity. Those organizations tend to view PPM practice or function closely linked with executive vision and annual goal setting as well as for many of these organizations, the process is tied to the annual budget cycle, business strategy and priority of initiatives. While the PMO may be viewed in some organization as the entity that oversees delivery of projects and reports results into the PPM function for benefit realization. Some of the names for these functions might be as: Corporate Governance Office, Corporate Project Governance, Center of Excellence, or Enterprise Strategy Services, Corporate Portfolio Management, etc.

In this controversy the physical split or consolidation of a function should not be the main focus, the focus should be more on the alignment and achieving corporate objectives as well as the handover process, and communication between the entities.

Some the questions organizations need to ask when linking PMO to PPM are:

- What is best strategy to link or unlink PPM to PMO
- What are the short term vs. long term benefits
- How is handover planned between the two functions
- Who is responsible for selection, execution, and closing of projects

Chapter Summary

In this chapter, the reader has been presented with some of the PMO controversies, to outsource or insource, is PMO temporary or permanent function, where does PPM function reside with PMO or separate. In the next chapter, these topics will be used to further illustrate how organizations deal with these controversies through case studies.

CHAPTER 7

PMO Case Studies

Case Study Introduction

This chapter will introduce four case studies that will cover the points that were covered in chapter eight and look at the practices the participants of the case studies do. In particular pertaining to:

- PMO vs. Project management
- PMO temporary vs. permanent
- PMO outsourcing vs. insourcing
- PMO and PPM relation

The multiple case studies represent different industries and organization size

- The first case is conducted in the financial insurance industry —Aviva Canada.
- The second case is conducted in the financial investment industry —INVEST&WEALTH.
- The Third case is conducted in the financial debit industry —Interac
- The fourth case is conducted in the food and beverage industry —McDonald's Canada
- Lastly, the fifth case is conducted in the game and entertainment industry—(G&E)

The analysis is broken into two sections: general analysis and specific case studies analysis. General analysis section is targeted to share general description to each case, similarities, and differences before detailing each case study. The specific case studies analysis covers details pertaining to the four practices. A total of 10 interviews conducted in total with all case studies participants.

General Analysis

Semi-structured interviews were used to collect initial data on the type, functions and expected benefits of the model chosen. Three groups of questions were included in the interview outline (see Appendix E) for details.

The first group of questions focused on obtaining general information on the respective organizations, their practices, structure, background to project management, and challenges. The second group of questions addresses the four practices and inquires about whether they had project management practice before PMO, or PMO has created the project practice; whether PMO was a temporary or a permanent function; whether the PMO insourced or outsourced, and whether the PPM practice is part of the PMO or a separate function from the PMO. The third and last group of questions address the sustainability elements and the impact on perceived value-add.

Table 6.1: Organizations Cases descriptions and participants

Organization Case	Brief Description	Participants	Interview Requested / Conducted
Aviva Canada	- Industry—Insurance - Purpose—Property and Casualty (P&C), Life, Annuity and Pension Funds - Organization—Matrix with focus on delivery through project initiatives	PMO head	3/3
INVEST& WEALTH	- Industry—Financial Investment - Purpose—investment solutions and advisory services - Organization—Matrix with focus on delivery through project initiatives	PMO head	2/2
Interac	- Industry—Financial payment - Purpose—National Payment network - Organization—Matrix with focus on product development through project initiatives	PMO Head	2/2
McDonald's	- Industry—Food Services / Restaurants - Purpose—Increase line of business, and increase franchisee profitability. - Organization—Matrix with focus on delivery through project initiatives	PMO Head	3/3

| G&E | - Industry—Gaming and Entertainment
- Purpose—Entertainment and gaming
- Organization—Matrix with focus on delivery through project initiatives | CGO head | 2/2 |

The selected cases had common characteristics such as multiple stakeholders with similar organization structure—Matrix and project delivery plays a major part in structuring internal cross functional initiatives. Further, they all have project management practices whether formal or informal prior to setting up and building their PMO's. The selected cases differ in the type of industries they are in, PMO structure and mandate. Among the many drivers to build PMO's, the main driver for each company to building PMO function is to improve standards and consistency across the organization whether the PMO is an ITPMO, EPMO, etc. The triggers and drivers might be different, the desired outcomes across all cases are: improved project delivery, consistency, quality, and value-add.

Specific Case Studies Analysis

Following the advice of Yin (1994, p. 128), *"a smart investigator will begin to compose the case study report even before data collection and analysis has been completed."* Following this advice, each case study will be reported using a standardized format that loosely follows the flow of the semi-structured interview as follows:

- Description of the case organization
- Description of their four practices
- Sustainability elements and value-add
- Benefits and Summary

The results which will be detailed in the next section show that all case studies have shown that project management must exist even in its basic forms and can be informal practice prior to having the need to create a PMO. While the case organizations have differed in the status of their PMO. Some PMO were created to be temporary, others were created to be permanent in nature. Some organizations have both temporary and permanent, while others have started as temporary and moved to permanent. None of the cases below is fully outsources, they ranged between hybrid to insourced models. Some organizations have outsourced some functions, and kept other functions insourced. As for PPM, almost all cases have PPM embedded in the PMO except for one case was PPM is a separate function.

A summary table illustrates the general findings described in the section above. After the general description, in the next section, all case studies will be detailed in-depth following similar structure detailing the four practices for each.

Table 6.2: Summary of the four practices in each organization

The Case Organization	PMO vs. Project management	Temporary vs. Permanent	Outsourcing vs. Insourcing	PMO vs. PPM
Aviva Canada	Project Management	Permanent / Temporary	Hybrid	PPM within PMO
INVEST& WEALTH	Project Management	Permanent	Insourcing	PPM within PMO

Interac	Project Management	Permanent	Insourcing	PPM within PMO
McDonald's	Project Management	Temporary / Permanent	Hybrid	PPM within PMO
G&E	Project Management	Permanent	Hybrid	PPM outside PMO

The Case Organizations

Aviva Canada

Description of the Aviva Canada Organization

Aviva Canada is one of the leading Property and Casualty insurance groups in Canada providing home, automobile, recreational vehicle, group and business insurance to more than three million customers. The Company is a wholly-owned subsidiary of UK-based Aviva Canada has 3,200 employees, 25 locations and 1,700 independent broker partners. Aviva Canada and its employees invest in positive change including through the Aviva Community Fund and Eva's Initiatives, its partner in Aviva's global Street to School program to help homeless and other at-risk youth reach their potential. http://Avivacanada.com/content/member-companies

Aviva Canada had multiple PMO's, where every PMO was potentially duplicating some efforts. Organization leaders were seeking efficiencies and consolidation of efforts as well as standardization across all functions. Hence, the concept of EPMO was born to denote the start of Enterprise wide PMO, one unit with one standard to methodology building, and project delivery. EPMO sits under the IT Organization, reporting to the EVP and CIO. EPMO is about 3 years old; before the consolidation they use to have 4 PMOs. EPMO consists of 60 people including contractors.

The EPMO is structured as a function, but operates in a projectized fashion. All staff are identified as part of the delivery (PGMgrs, PMs, PCs, BAs, and Sr. Project Financial Analysts) are assigned through the organizations demand and supply of initiatives. Once the delivery staff is assigned, the Program or Project Manager is then assigned to its Executive Sponsor and Project Owner where they temporarily report to them in a project structure. And for all escalations, issue resolutions, and their own respective development and reporting relationship, they continue to report to their line managers. More precisely: AVP, Portfolio Management and Delivery for the PGMgrs, PMs and PCs, then the Sr Mgr Business Analysis for the BAs, and then the Mgr EPMO Finance for the SPFAs.

The head of EPMO for Aviva Canada started being accountable for Portfolio Management, Planning, Reporting and Delivery, in addition to Enterprise Resource Pool Management, QA & Compliance, and Portfolio Risk Management. All Project Managers, Project Coordinators, and Business Analysts report into the head of the EPMO.

Table 6.3: Summary of Aviva Canada Organization (Canada)

Organization Characteristics	Details
Ownership	Public
Industry	Insurance
Size	Large (3,200 employees)

Organization	Matrix with focus on delivery through project initiatives
Culture	Rewards in job security and benefits of long term employment. Niche specialized long term projects
Competition	Intact-AXA, Co-Operators, Wawanesa
Strategy for growth	Two pillars: A Great Underwriting Company. Committed to the Broker Channel.

Description of Aviva Canada's four (4) practices:

Project management was practiced prior to having EPMO; as a matter of fact there were four PMO's and one of the EPMO mandates was to consolidate the various PMO's. Project management as a practice existed before EPMO at Aviva Canada and what motivated the creation of EPMO in addition to consolidation are the unification of standards in methodology, reporting, and opportunities to better assess demand management across the organization.

1. PMO vs. Project Management

Project management was practiced at Aviva Canada prior to having PMO's. Then separate PMO's were created to promote the delivery of project management. Finally EPMO existed to consolidate and improve standards of effectiveness. In general, project management was practiced at large prior to building PMO's.

2. Temporary or Permanent

The EPMO is a permanent function and prior to it the four PMO's were permanent functions within their organizations. The drivers for a permanent PMO are the size of budget, resources, complexity, and ambiguity of indicators. Further, allow Aviva Canada to tailor processes and governance to fit organization structure and culture. Although the EPMO is permanent, there are specific PMO mandates around large and complex initiatives (i.e. program), the PMO with the program structure can be required. For example, if one Program Lead with multiple project stream, executive sponsors, business owner's and vendors coming together as one delivery management team is critical for success. This setup also allows tailoring enterprise assets and processes to be fit for need, within agreed boundaries. Just like the initiative that has a start and end date, the PMO within a program is dismantled once the initiative is completed.

3. Outsourcing vs. Insourcing

EPMO within Aviva Canada is mainly insourced. PMO outsourcing isn't considered because of the EPMO reach and its strategic nature. However, the model EPMO uses to maximize benefits from various resources and functions within PMO led through hybrid model. Project resource loaded is assessed and assigned to projects as required with contractors. PPM Administration hybrid (i.e. Level 1 request outsourced, Level 2+ insourced). PPM tools are outsourced (SaaS). Contractor Management and sourcing outsourced. Project managers are insourced, others outsourced. Training and career development is outsourced to career development as well as in-house on the job training programs. Everyone has 70 / 20 / 10 personal development plan. More precisely when it comes to learning, 70% is on-the-job-training through assignment and involvement in other activities, 20% provided externally, 10% that is self-initiated.

4. Project Portfolio Management ("PPM") vs. PMO

PPM resides within EPMO and is not a separate function. PPM sits in EPMO—to ensure project to program to portfolio linkages; leveraging SaaS offering to streamline planning and reporting. PMO assumes the responsibility of PPM planning and prioritization, and reviewing monthly results with executives. The main important drivers for having PPM embedded within the PMO are: based on the strategic position of the; additionally, PMO is set at the C level and there are no other functions that do similar work and all described functions report into the head of EPMO. The benefit is centralizing the PPM under one governance structure and better collaboration on handover between the functions relating to projects.

Sustainability elements and value-add

PMO value-add was visible immediately with closing between 35 to 40 medium to large scale projects. All initiatives are reviewed and approved by Executive Committee. The portfolio is reviewed on a monthly basis with financial view of all initiatives. Tiered governance allowed for smooth decision making empowering employees at the various levels to make decisions. Visible capacity planning and transparency across the organization are major wins and value-add. EPMO value based was visible in the human resources value and customer value as in

a. HR factor: Full demand and supply view FTEs vs Contractors based on the project demand BoW (Book of Work). Tiered governance allows junior staff to be assigned to initiatives that match their skill sets and experiences. Support career path (i.e. PC to Jr PM to PM to Sr PM to PgMgr). Support company-wide expense challenge discussions (who are assigned to what—therefore, what initiative should stop).

b. Quality factor: BoW fully visible and transparent, refreshed every month. Status and progress rolled up monthly to a portfolio view—"Step to Green" for Amber and Red initiatives published and visible

Dollars: budget vs actual vs forecast always available, hence, where resources ($, people, assets) are consumed always transparent. CAR and PAR issued to project core management team; they are tracked against employees' personal objectives—tying to their respective bonus structure.

c. Delivery factor: Because of transparency, and because employees can't work on initiatives that are not approved, throughout has increased as a result of having reduced the 'work-in-the-dark' projects.
RAG status well understood by everyone; four dimensions to RAG—two objectives and two subjective. Objective: Cost is derived from CPI, and schedule derived from SPI. Subjective: Resources and Scope. Overall RAG: two ambers, overall amber. One red, overall red.

d. Cost factor: Dollars in budget vs actual vs forecast always available. Hence, where resources ($, people, assets) are consumed always transparent.

<u>Benefits and Summary</u>

In summary, EPMO has achieved its objectives in consolidating PMO's, running a successful PPM and ability to apply hybrid models between outsourcing and insourcing were it best fits their needs. While EPMO is a permanent strategic function, there are temporary project functions that run large size and complex programs. Below is a summary of the benefits EPMO achieved.

Quantitative:

- Portfolio is able to deliver around 10-15% below plan every year because of strong financial management, status and progress

visibility company-wide, and re-assign FT resources to work contractors are assigned to (reducing the premium we need to pay as a result of using a contractor).
- Contractor to FTE ratio is about 1:4; managing their corporate knowledge as a critical asset (to not go beyond 30%).
- Delivering 35-40 change initiatives per year—consistently for the past three years (inclusive of present).
- Using "one" Managed Service Provider for all contractor needs has reduced Aviva Canada's total contractor spending by 20%.

Qualitative:

- Benefits realization embedded—on closeout activities, finance business partners update respective business unit cost center.
- Motivated staff as everyone is aware of the change agenda.
- Attract talent throughout the organization as people want to be part of the success stories.
- Country—Regional—Global Portfolio roll-ups available; create synergies across the globe on similar initiatives.

INVEST&WEALTH

Description of the INVEST&WEALTH Organization

INVEST&WEALTH is a wealth management company. Headquartered in Toronto, Canada, and, through our partners and subsidiaries, have huge presence North America and Europe. INVEST&WEALTH creates and provides investment solutions and advisory services for financial advisors, institutions, corporations and foundations through our two main businesses: investment management and financial advisory.

INVEST&WEALTH's operations are carried out through various divisions and brands, each of which capitalizes on a specific financial services segment. This specialization allows each division to focus on its strengths, while retaining the flexibility to leverage expertise in other divisions in order to provide a complete wealth management solution for clients.

INVEST&WEALTH did not have a PMO 5 years ago, prior to that time project management was practiced informally and inconsistent manner. Organization growth demanded efficiencies and standardization; hence, the concept of a centralized PMO was born to centralize project management practices across all IT functions. Today INVEST&WEALTH PMO is 5 years old, with 10 projects managers, and 2 project officers and reports into investment executive.

The ITPMO is structured as a function, but operates in a projectized fashion. All project managers indentified as part of the delivery are assigned by ITPMO Head through our demand and supply of initiatives. The head of PMO was hired to set-up, build-out, and sustain the operation of the ITPMO. In this new structure, all project managers who were in the organization and newly hired project managers report into the PMO.

Table 6.4: Summary of INVEST&WEALTH Organization

Organization Characteristics	Details
Ownership	Public
Industry	Investments
Size	Large 1000+ employees
Organization	Matrix with focus on delivery through project initiatives
Culture	Rewards in job security and benefits of long term employment.
Competition	Other investment firms
Strategy for growth	Mergers and Acquisitions

Description of INVEST&WEALTH's four (4) practices:

Project management was practiced prior to having ITPMO, but it was informal. There was no clear differentiator between a project manager's role and a business analyst. The roles were mixed-up. The challenge was clear accountability as well as standard methodology, and consistency across all projects.

1. PMO vs. Project Management

Project management was practiced at INVEST&WEALTH prior to having ITPMO's. The challenge was lack of consistency or repeatable processes which meant success of delivery is dependent on project managers' skill set. Then five years ago a formal ITPMO's was created with the mandate to set standards, build methodology, oversee delivery, provide training, and establish a formal project managers career path. to promote the delivery of project management. It took two years for IT PMO to become stabilized and sustained. In general, project management was practiced at large prior to building ITPMO and having the PMO was more of formalizing the practice.

2. Temporary or Permanent

The ITPMO was set to be a permanent function from the beginning. The intend of the leadership and the mandate that the PMO head carried was to create a CoE in charge of standards, delivery, methodology, and training. Project management was to become a core skill for IT, many other IT functions are encouraged to attend project management training. Smaller projects by ITPMO definitions those that are contained within a business unit are often run by the business unit itself in which they are expected to follow project management rigor without having a project manager leading the project. While there is no temporary PMO, there are projects that are run outside of PMO as mentioned above.

3. Outsourcing vs. Insourcing

ITPMO within INVEST&WEALTH is mainly insourced. PMO outsourcing isn't considered because of the strategic position of the IT PMO and being a CoE for the organization. Project managers mainly full time, there are 15% of contractors or on-demand resources based on specific domain knowledge required, or high demand for project work; hence, contractors are demand based and skills based. In the set-up and build-out stage a SaaS model was used for the purpose of immediate centralization and consolidation of project managers and demand management. After the first stage, EPM Project server was procured as internal platform to improve demand management, centralized project planning, BI reporting, and PPM streamlining.

4. Project Portfolio Management ("PPM") vs. PMO

PPM resides within ITPMO and is not a separate function. PPM sits in ITPMO—to ensure project to program to portfolio linkages. ITPMO is involved in the executive annual planning and assumes the responsibility of PPM planning and prioritization, and reviewing monthly results with executives. The main important drivers for having PPM embedded within the ITPMO are: based on the strategic position of the PMO, PMO is a knowledge house and mature entity in the organization so it was logical to house the PPM planning; and PMO ensures that projects requests can be centralized across all business units.

Sustainability elements and value-add

PMO value-add was visible immediately with closing close to 18 medium to large scale projects. All initiatives are reviewed and approved by Executive Committee. PPM process is reviewed on a monthly basis. In addition, consistency in reporting, managing projects, and repeatability of process, improved project quality and speed of delivery. Visible capacity planning and transparency across the organization are major wins and value-add. ITPMO value based was visible in the human resources value and customer value as in

a. HR factor: Full demand and supply view FTEs allows organization to well plan capacity and deal with on-demand through contractors. Continuous training improves adoption and acceptance of PMO across the organization. Formalizing project managers role and establishing career path and investing in training, improve retention rates and morale. Training and certification improve specialized skill sets and provide variety on the job.

b. Quality factor: consistency and standardization improve planning quality, results quality, and process quality. The quality of information has improved as a result which allow for better decision making ability. Budget vs actual vs forecast always available, hence, where resources ($, people, assets) are consumed always transparent. ITPMO became the central function for delivering projects and business units do not kick-off projects without ensuring ITPMO has assigned a project manager

c. Delivery factor: Because of transparency, consistency, qualified project managers, and predictability; initiatives delivery rate has improved.

d. Cost factor: Dollars in budget vs actual vs forecast always available. Hence, where resources ($, people, assets) are consumed always transparent. Total cost savings from well staffing initiatives with current project managers has at least tripled the savings.

Benefits and Summary

In summary, ITPMO has achieved its objectives running a successful PPM, skilled project managers and ability to improve performance based on feedback loop to improve in the areas pointed out. Below is a summary of the benefits ITPMO achieved.

Quantitative:

- Improving portfolio planning 10-15% annually as a result of strong resource management analysis, financial management, and visibility of all projects company-wide.
- Contractor to FTE ratio, only 15% contactors. Managing corporate knowledge as a critical asset (to not go beyond 15%).
- Delivering 35-40 initiatives per year—consistently for the past four years (inclusive of present).

Qualitative:

- Benefits realization embedded—on closeout activities, finance business partners update respective business unit cost center.
- Motivated staff throughout the organization as people want to be part of the success stories
- Attract talent, as all project managers are being invested into through training and career path development.

Interac

Description of Interac Association

Interac Association (the "Association" or "Organization") is a recognized leader in debit card services. The Association is responsible for the development and operations of the Inter-Member Network (IMN), a national payment network that allows Canadians to access their money through Automated Banking Machines and Point-of-Sale terminals across Canada. Formed in 1984, the Association is now composed of a diverse group of members, including banks, trust companies, credit unions, caisses populaires, merchants, and technology and payment related companies. Today, Canadians coast to coast associate the INTERAC® brand with leading electronic payment services that are trusted, secure and reliable. The Association is a not-for-profit organization, governed by a 14-Member Board of Directors, appointed annually based on the business sector and the volume of transactions processed. More information about Interac Association may be accessed at http://www.interac.ca

The Organization, which has grown tremendously in recent years in terms of budget, number of employees and number of initiatives, is matrix in structure. In particular, all business units of the Organization work in a functional manner and are organized around major competencies (Product, IT, Sales, Legal, Compliance & Regulations, etc.). The Organization continuously seeks to improve its product offerings to continue to compete with other payment networks and to offer better service to Canadians. With these objectives in mind, the Association astutely identified the need to organize its delivery of new or enhanced product offerings in a projectized fashion to keep up with increased initiative demand and to deliver on associated commitments. As a result, the Organization's executive management decided to create a project practice to address these demands among other challenges and needs including the following: increased project load and need to commit to project delivery; need for increased insight into capacity and demand management planning; and the need for objective project prioritization based on specific measures. The Organization also recognized that a lack of standardization could have led to unnecessarily prolonged planning cycles which could have negatively impacted its ability to take advantage of potential opportunities and its credibility.

In summary, it became prudent to introduce (i) more rigors to manage both Organization wide and individual initiatives and (ii) a standard method of delivery starting with the right project selection criteria. Accordingly, the Organization's executive champion initiated a needs analysis and assessment of requirements to find the right skills to build a Project Management Office ("PMO") practice and to obtain buy-in from the executive committee.

Table 6.5: Summary of the Organization

Organization Characteristics	Details
Ownership	Not for profit
Industry	Financial—Debit payment
Size	Small 120 employees
Organization	Matrix with focus on delivery through project initiatives
Culture	Rewards in job security and benefits of long term employment. Niche specialized long term projects.
Competition	Other payment networks
Strategy for growth	Mainly organic with focus on core business. Two pillars: Core product growth New business expansion

The new PMO is structured as a function, but operates in a projectized manner with a total of five (5) project managers, two (2) of which report into the PMO with the other three (3) reporting to their respective business areas. There is also one (1) process and tools specialist and the PMO head. The PMO in turn reports directly into the Organization's Enterprise Strategy Department that reports into the CEO's office. The PMO reporting structure was established in this manner because it allows the PMO to sit at the corporate level to streamline project delivery and ensures consistency of this delivery across all other functions. In addition, this structure was established to ensure no conflict of interest between the PMO and any particular business unit or units as the enterprise function drives strategic goals for the Organization that touch all business units.

The PMO was set-up and built-out with the goal of being a centre for project excellence and a permanent function to serve the Organization. Prior to establishing the PMO, the Organization did not have formal project practices, although informal project management was visible. More specifically, some large impact initiatives were run as projects and were complemented by consultants and internal staff. Formalized project practices also existed in the client implementations area.

<u>Description of the Organization's Four (4) Practices:</u>

Project management at the Organization was lightly practiced and mainly informal. Prior to having a PMO, there were some formal attempts to structure implementations work or requirements work within one business unit which sometimes widened the gap between business units. The PMO was expected to build project management practices along with hiring project management professionals and implementing processes and supporting tools. The PMO was also given the charge to build strategic initiatives alignment. Since the Organization did not have formal project management practices, the PMO existed to create these practices. Organizations often benefit when they identify the need to have project management to structure project delivery and when they are able to formalize it as early on as possible. As a result, such organizations put the requisite practices in place and grow discipline in a standard manner.

1. PMO vs. Project Management

Despite the vague and light project management practice at the Organization, project management elements did exist. That being said, the PMO was required to broaden the project management vision and to formalize the supporting practices. Although the Association is small in size, its reputation, impact, and reach in the market is substantial; hence, the need for a sustainable entity to become the custodian of project management practice.

2. Temporary or Permanent

When the PMO was charted to be built, the vision was not to have a temporary function surrounding a particular project, but more of a strategic corporate function to oversee the delivery and alignment of executive initiatives based on board direction and internal capacity. The decision was to have a permanent in-house department reporting into the Enterprise Strategy Department which in turn reports to the CEO. The positioning of the PMO and the permanent nature of it were the two elements that provided success to the Organization's PMO. First they ensured neutrality and executive presence oversight in governance. Second, they ensured adherence to set processes and standards. Finally, centralized ownership allowed the PMO to drive and audit the performance of the project portfolio assets and project delivery. In addition, some of the resistance and challenges in introducing the PMO function would likely not have been appropriately addressed unless there was a PMO on the ground overseeing the project practices and ensuring value-add. This resulted in the Organization making the position permanent to continue with the sustainability journey.

3. Outsourcing vs. Insourcing

The set-up, build-out and ongoing sustainability of Association's PMO is completely owned by the Organization. As an essential function that oversees the Organization's project portfolio assets; the knowledge being provided by the PMO needed to stay in-house. The PMO was built as a full time function to ensure continuity in building and honing the standards and supporting framework. Establishing the PMO as a full time function resulted in better compliance and internal adoption and ownership. Project managers however, are insourced and outsourced depending on projects and capacity planning. There are functional managers as well who are trained as project managers to manage certain initiatives.

4. Project Portfolio Management ("PPM") vs. PMO

PPM practice is a corner stone in the PMO build-out. Establishing the PMO at the strategic level meant that the PMO encompassed the PPM function. It also meant that the PMO was responsible for the main functions of project delivery, methodology and processes, tools and training, project resource management, and portfolio management. The main important drivers for having PPM embedded within the PMO were the following: the Organization's small size (based on the size of the Organization a separate function was not required); the PMO's strategic level placement (the PMO was set at the enterprise level); there were no other functions that do Portfolio identification and selection; and all described functions reported into the head of PMO. The benefits to embedding PPM in the PMO included centralizing PPM under one governance structure, and better collaboration when handing over the associated functions relating to projects.

Sustainability Elements and Value-add

The PMO value-add was visible in the early stages of set-up and build-out when standards reporting brought in comparable pictures of project health checks, project traffic light colors, and standard templates helped project managers and stakeholders set the right expectations and read the information and measures in similar manner which improved collaboration and minimized interpretations. The PMO value-add was visible in the human resources value and customer value as outlined in the bullet points below.

- a. HR Factor: Full project demand management. Training and rollout of standards and processes helped improve adoption. Project manager career path and centralization of artifacts added value and contributed to the PMO's sustainability.

- b. Quality Factor: The improvement in quality of data and accuracy of project planning, tracking of project status, and execution enforced a higher level of quality that also contributed to the PMO's sustainability journey. Complete transparency in projects with guidance on color coding projects depending on health of golden triangle. Executives actively involved in taking action and holding their teams accountable to ensure projects stay on track.

- c. Delivery Factor: The PMO sustains performance through annual goals and objectives from senior leadership, that is translated in the PMO roadmap and direction which itself includes required updates, additions, and changes. While new components might be integrated, their integration is based on leadership thought process and they are neither radical in nature, nor transformational, but build on successful foundation from the set-up and build-out, to ensure the sustainability and growth of the PMO.

- d. Cost Factor: Improving alignment cycle of annual budget planning and estimation and projection of the cost of initiatives keeps all project funding visible. This area is still evolving as the Organization continues to be time and resource conscious and cost has recently played a major factor in justifying and measuring the success of projects.

Benefits and Summary

The PMO was sought by the Organization from its top level to formally establish standards and strategic drive for the Organizations' initiatives. Hence the PMO needed to be in-sourced. Below is a summary of the quantitative and qualitative benefits the PMO achieved for the Organization.

Quantitative:

- Improved PPM turn around by full quarter, closing on all approved prioritized projects before a fiscal year kick-off;
- Improved annual resource estimations and projections by 50% through alignment of initiative and resources;
- Improved project planning by 50% through standard project rigor. All enterprise initiatives have a charter, project plan, resource plan, resource planning, and standard report; and
- Delivered (and will continue to deliver) 15-25 initiatives per year with complete transparency to all initiatives.

Qualitative:

- Improved morale as teams' awareness of the big picture and projects continues to progress;
- Improved alignment and quantification of business demands and improved value-add to the business;

- Improved ability to track and understand the progress of projects throughout the project life cycle which resulted in complete transparency into project reporting; and

McDonald's—Canada

Description of the McDonald Organization

McDonald's is the world's leading foodservice retailer, with more than 33,000 local restaurants serving over 64 million people in 119 countries every day. Today, 2.5 million guests visit our restaurants across Canada every day. With its Canadian franchisees, McDonald's Restaurants of Canada Limited owns and operates more than 1,400 restaurants and employs more than 80,000 Canadians coast-to-coast. Approximately 75% of McDonald's Canadian restaurants are locally owned and operated by independent entrepreneurs in communities from coast to coast.

- McDonald's Canada is lucky to be part of the lives of millions of Canadians in communities across the country, helping to build a strong workforce, business partnerships and local economies.
- When both direct and indirect employment impacts are taken together, McDonald's Canada creates more than 200,000 jobs, generating almost $4.5 billion in local annual economic activity
- McDonald's Canada is the largest buyer of ground beef in the Canadian restaurant industry with annual purchases of more than 66 million pounds
- McDonald's Canada contributes approximately $75 million in payroll taxes and benefits and $34 million in business taxes nationally

- Overall, McDonald's Canada creates more than $610 million annually in taxes through the generation of new jobs and additional purchases of goods and services from other Canadian businesses

McDonald's is a global organization that has multiple PMO's in various countries focused on delivery; The ITPMO Canada is structured as a function, but operates in a projectized fashion to manage the demand and supply of initiatives.

Table 6.6: Summary of McDonald's Organization (Canada)

Organization Characteristics	Details
Ownership	Public
Industry	Food Services—Restaurants
Size	Large (77,000 employee)
Organization	Matrix with focus on delivery through project initiatives
Culture	Employees' retention, one of 50 best employers to work for past 9 years.
Competition	Other coffee shops and restaurants in similar type of business
Strategy for growth	Two pillars: Increase line of business. Increase franchisee profitability.

Description of McDonald's four (4) practices:

Project management was practiced prior to having ITPMO; however, it was informal and only rigors is around large projects were project management discipline and project managers were outsourced to perform specific isolated large project. Project management as a practice existed before ITPMO at McDonald's and what motivated the creation of standards in methodology, reporting, and opportunities to better assess demand management across the organization.

1. PMO vs. Project Management

Project management was practiced at McDonald's prior to having ITPMO. It was recognized formally after a huge success in a large initiative, namely the implementation of the gift card project when management and executives recognized the success was due to project management discipline and recognized the internal need to carry on similar projects and that provided the business case for a central CoE. In general, project management was practiced at large prior to building PMO's.

2. Temporary or Permanent

PMO started out as temporary for a large organizational project and not until the success of Gift Card Implementation in 2006 were the need for having a permanent function emerged. This temporary PMO never faded after the project was delivered and became the first delivery PMO and resided in IT. The function has since moved from being temporary in nature to permanent.

3. Outsourcing vs. Insourcing

ITPMO within McDonald's is mainly in sourced. PMO outsourcing isn't considered because of the ITPMO reach and its strategic nature. However, the model ITPMO uses to maximize benefits from various resources and functions within PMO led through mainly insourcing, with occasional outsourcing based on supply and demand.

4. PPM vs. PMO

PPM resides within ITPMO and is not a separate function. PPM sits in ITPMO—to ensure project to program to portfolio linkages. The main important drivers for having PPM embedded within the PMO are: based on the strategic position of the PMO. The benefit is centralizing the PPM under one governance structure and better collaboration on handover between the functions relating to projects.

Sustainability elements and value-add

PMO value-add was visible immediately with closing close to 12-18 medium to large scale projects. All initiatives are reviewed and approved by Executive Committee. PPM process is reviewed on a monthly basis with financial view of all initiatives. Tiered governance allowed for smooth decision making empowering employees at the various levels to make decisions. Visible capacity planning and transparency across the organization are major wins and value-add. ITPMO value based was visible in the human resources value and customer value as in

   a. HR factor: Full demand and supply view FTEs vs Contractors based on the project demand. Bridging skill set gaps, and looking to retain FTE's for growth of skills and ensure continuity of key projects. Tiered governance allows junior staff to be assigned to initiatives that match their skill sets and experiences as well as enabled their knowledge of what, when, and to whom to escalate to. Support career path and promote within.

   b. Quality factor: Project progress and color status indication project health have standard definition. Transparent status reports that are refreshed every month. Simple Metrics are put in place to ensure projects deliver on the Quality standards they have been chartered for.

c. Delivery factor: Because of transparency, and because PMO's ability to be involved in strategic planning and assigning PM's for prioritized projects, there is focus on employees can't work on initiatives that are not approved, throughout has increased as a result of having reduced unassigned projects.

d. Cost factor: Manage baseline budget, track cost of internal resources and keep vendors on track Hence, where resources ($, people, assets) are consumed always transparent.

<u>Benefits and Summary</u>

In summary McDonald's Canada ITPMO has achieved its objectives building a delivery focus PMO that improved transparency, governance, reporting, standards, and retaining skilled project staff. Below is a summary of the benefits EPMO achieved

Quantitative:

- Portfolio is able to deliver within plan every year because of strong financial management, status and progress visibility company-wide.
- Contractor to FTE ratio is about 1:4; managing our corporate knowledge as a critical asset
- Delivering 12-18 medium to large initiatives—consistently for the past five years

Qualitative:

- Motivated staff as everyone is aware of the change agenda.
- Attract talent throughout the organization as people want to be part of the success stories.

- Country—Regional—Global Portfolio roll-ups available; create synergies across the globe on similar initiatives.

G&E—Game & Entertainment

Description of the (G&E) Organization

(G&E) is an Operational Enterprise Agency with its affiliated companies employs more than 5000 people throughout the country. G&E's vision is to be a role model for gaming entertainment worldwide through the variety of their entertainment options. G&E's mission is to make life better for people through entertainment products that generate substantial employment opportunities, and provide services to the community programs such programs as health care, promoting physical fitness, sport, recreation and cultural activities.

G&E project management background had multiple PMO's throughout the years. An EPMO was setup many years ago with focus on processes as a priority and secondary focus on delivery. The result was improved processes, but delivery required more efforts to improve as expected. Therefore, the organization realized that immediate attention is required to streamline initiatives and focus on delivery. EPMO reported into IT as well which limited the reach to the corporate initiatives alignment and limited their domain. As a result corporate governance was required to oversee project delivery and portfolio planning through Corporate Governance Office (CGO).

The head of CGO was hired to run PMO and PPM reporting into the business C level executive. CGO today is a mature organization with over 50 employees between heads of PMO and PPM, project managers, and project officers and it is about two years old. CGO is structured as a function, but operates in a projectized fashion. All staff identified as part of the project delivery, are assigned through organization demand and supply of initiatives. Once the delivery project manager is assigned, the project follow and adhere to a structure with focus on measuring delivery and commitments holding project team and project sponsor accountable for the milestones identified. The PPM head is involved throughout the lifecycle to understand the value of an initiative and determine if an initiative needs to stop and another starts, while the PMO head focus on delivering the assigned initiative per the priority sequence provided

Table 6.7: Summary of G&E Organization

Organization Characteristics	Details
Ownership	Public
Industry	Entertainment
Size	Large
Organization	Matrix with focus on delivery through project initiative
Culture	Rewards in job security and benefits of long term employment.
Competition	Other entertainments including online
Strategy for growth	Revenue generation that feeds into community projects, and improving client experience

Description of G&E's four (4) practices:

Project management was practiced prior to having CGO; as a matter of fact there were various PMO's including an EPMO. Project management as a practice existed before CGO at G&E and what motivated the creation of CGO is the focus on delivery and alignment over the focus on processes. In addition to consolidation of project managers and unification of standards across the organization, CGO had delivery accountability and centralization of project management activities. PMO within CGO today focuses 75% delivery and 25% process which provide the PMO the proper ratio to focus on delivery and utilize the standard process to ensure consistency in measuring delivery success.

1. PMO vs. Project Management

Project management was practiced at G&E prior to having PMO's. Then separate PMO's were created to promote the delivery of project management, project delivery was decentralized and every area owned their delivery which resulted in underutilized resources and budget were exceeded. Finally CGO existed to consolidate and improve standards of effectiveness and improve corporate delivery as well as centralize project managers and project management practices. In general, project management was practiced at large prior to building PMO's concluding with CGO.

2. Temporary or Permanent

Throughout the PMOs journey at G&E, none of them were built on the premise of being a temporary or around a specific project. There has been many PMO's and there was decentralization of delivery; hence, accountability was an issue. CGO is a CoE and a permanent function that resides at the corporate level. The drivers for a permanent function are the size of budget, resources, complexity, and ambiguity of indicators. Further, allow G&E to tailor processes and governance to fit organization's structure and culture.

3. Outsourcing vs. Insourcing

CGO within G&E is mainly insourced. PMO outsourcing isn't considered because of the CGO's reach and its strategic nature. However, there are contractors that are leveraged throughout the organization to balance the project supply and demand. Project managers are mainly insourced and report into CGO through CoE function. Training and career development is hybrid were there are internally supported for career development and advancements and on the job training; in addition, some professional developments are outsourced.

4. Project Portfolio Management ("PPM") vs. PMO

PMO and PPM are two separate functions at G&E and both functions report into CGO. While PMO is focused on project delivery, PPM is focused on portfolio management throughout the fiscal year. The hand over from PPM to PMO occurs between the two areas when a project in the PPM that is approved is ready to start, it is handed then to PMO that runs it till completion. PMO in return runs the project keeping PPM with status and progress and another major hand shake is expected at the project closing to PPM for benefit realization.

The main important drivers for having PPM separate from PMO are: based on the strategic position of the CGO and to keep the accountability and focus for every area; additionally, CGO is set at the C level and ensures collaboration and synergy between the PMO and PPM functions. The benefit is centralizing the PPM and PMO under one governance structure and better collaboration on handover between the functions relating to projects evaluated and prioritized at the PPM cycle, then handed over for execution and delivery.

<u>Sustainability elements and value-add</u>

PMO value-add was visible immediately with closing close to 40 medium to large scale projects. All initiatives are reviewed and approved by Executive Committee. PPM process is reviewed on a monthly basis with financial view of all initiatives. Tiered governance allowed for smooth decision making empowering employees at the various levels to make decisions. Visible capacity planning and transparency across the organization are major wins and value-add. EPMO value based was visible in the human resources value and customer value as in

a. HR factor: Full demand and supply view FTEs vs Contractors based on the project demand and supply. Tiered governance allows junior staff to be assigned to initiatives that match their skill sets and experiences. Support career path (i.e. PC to Jr PM to PM to Sr PM to PgMgr). Allow resources to understand organization project load through transparency in initiatives. Further, project managers, know who's assigned to what, and when and why initiatives should stop).

b. Quality factor: PPM is fully visible and transparent, updated monthly. Status and progress rolled up monthly to a portfolio view—"Step to Green" for Amber and Red initiatives published and visible
Dollars: budget vs actual vs forecast always available, hence, where resources ($, people, assets) are consumed always transparent.

c. Delivery factor: Because of transparency, and because employees can't work on initiatives that are not approved, throughout has increased as a result of having reduced the 'work-in-the-dark' projects. Further with emphasis on delivery 75% and on process 25%, the mantra for the CGO is use the process, not just follow the process. This has improved the visibility, accountability, and the end results more projects are delivered.

d. Cost factor: Improve dollars in budget vs actual vs forecast always available. Hence, where resources ($, people, assets) are consumed always transparent.

<u>Benefits and Summary</u>

In summary, CGO has achieved organization objectives through focusing the two areas into specific accountability, while PPM worked the portfolio priority, monitoring and control, PMO focused on executing on these prioritized initiatives. CGO is a permanent function that is in-house with occasional outsourcing for skills and talent to manage the resource utilization based on project supply and demand. Below is a summary of the benefits EPMO achieved.

Quantitative:

- Portfolio is able to deliver around 20% below plan every year because of strong financial management, status and progress visibility company-wide, and re-assign FT resources to work contractors are assigned to (reducing the premium we need to pay as a result of using a contractor).
- Delivering 35-40 change initiatives per year—consistently for the past three years (inclusive of present).
- Biggest win was increase number of milestones in 3 month duration from 22% to 72%

Qualitative:

- Benefits realization embedded—on closeout activities, finance business partners update respective business unit cost center.
- Motivated staff as everyone is aware of the change agenda.

- Portfolio roll-ups available; create synergies across the various business units on similar initiatives.
- Ability to improve accountability and focus across PPM and PMO

Chapter Summary

In this chapter, the reader has been presented with five case studies the results of PMO survey that highlighted the complexity of the PMOLC, and shed light on the nature of each phase, and the skills required to build each phase. Further illustrate similar and different challenges in each phase in the lifecycle

The results show that all case studies have shown that project management must exist even in its basic forms and can be informal practice prior to having the need to create a PMO. While the case organizations have differed in the status of their PMO. Some PMO were created to be temporary, others were created to be permanent in nature. Some organizations have both temporary and permanent, while others have started as temporary and moved to permanent. None of the cases below is fully outsources, they ranged between hybrid to insourced models. Some organizations have outsourced some functions, and kept other functions insourced. As for PPM, almost all cases have PPM embedded in the PMO except for one case was PPM is a separate function.

REFERENCES

Andersen, B., Henriksen, B., & Aarseth, W. (2007). Benchmarking of Project Management Office Establishment: Extracting Best Practices. Journal of Management in Engineering, 23(2), 97-104

Bolles, D. (2002). Building Project Management Centers of Excellence. New York: AMACOM.

Bowman, C. and Ambrosini, V. (2000), Value Creation Versus Value Capture: Towards a Coherent Definition of Value in Strategy. British Journal of Management, 11: 1-15. doi: 10.1111/1467-8551.00147)

Brown, D., & Wilson, S. (2005). The Black Book of Outsourcing: How to Manage the Changes, Challenges, and Opportunities. Wiley & Sons, Inc, USA

Crawford, J. K. (2001). Portfolio management: overview and best practices. Project management for business professionals: a comprehensive guide. J. Knutson. New York, NY, Wiley & Sons, Inc.

Crawford, J. K. (2002). The strategic project office. New York, NY, Marcel Dekker AG.

Desouza, K., Evaristo, R. (2006). Project management offices: A case study of knowledge-based archetypes. International Journal of Information Management, 26(5), 414-423.

Dinsmore, Paul. (2000). Project Office: Does one size fit all? PMNetwork 14(April): 27-29

Gareis, R. (2005). The management strategy of the project oriented company. Handbook of Management by projects, ed. Roland Gareis. MANZsche Verlags, Vienna, Page 35-47.

Gareis et al. (2011). Relating sustainability principles to managing projects: First reflections on a case study project. Proceedings for IRNOP 2011, Montreal, Canada.

Hoque, F., Samamurthy, V., Zmund, R., Trainer, T., Wilson,C. (2005). Winning The 3-Legged Race—When Business and Technology Run Together. Prentice Hall, New Jersy USA

H. Kwak., Dai, Yi., Xiao, C. (2000). Assessing the Value of Project Management Offices (PMO). PMI Research Conference 2000 Bates, 1998).

Hofer, C., Carton., R. (2006). Measuring Organizational Performance. Edward Elgar Publishing Limited, UK

Karkukly, W. (2011). An Investigation into outsourcing of PMO Functions for improved organizational performance: A quantitative and Qualitative study. Trafford Publishing, US & Canada.

Kerzner, H. (2004). *Advanced Project Management: Best Practices on Implementation, 2nd Edition. Wiley & Sons. Inc, USA*

Kerzner, H. (2005). *Project Management—AS system Approach to Planning, Scheduling, and Controlling.* Wiley & Sons, Inc, USA

Light, M., Berg, T. (2000). The project office: Teams, Processes and Tools. GartnerGroup RAS Services.

Paladino, B. (2007). Five Principles of Corporate Performance Management. John Wiley & Sons 2007

PM Solutions research. (2012), the state of the PMO"

Porter, M.E. (1985). Competitive Advantage, Free Press: New York.

Project Management Institute (PMI). (2004). A Guide to the Project Management Body of Knowledge, Third edition (PMBOK guide). Project Management Institute

Project Management Institute (PMI). (2008). A Guide to the Project Management Body of Knowledge, Fourth edition (PMBOK guide). Project Management Institute

Rad, Parviz., Levin, Ginger. (2002). The Advanced Project Management Office: A Comprehensive Look at Function and Implementation, CRC Press, 2002, ISBN: 1574443402

Santosus, M. (2003). Why you need a Project Management Office (PMO). Retrieved September, 2008 from http://www.cio.com/article/print/29887

Sekaran, U. (2003). Research methods for business: A skill building approach (4th ed.). Hoboken, NJ: John Wiley.

Simon, J. L., & Burstein, P. (1969). Basic research methods in social science (3rd ed.). New York: McGraw-Hill.

http://en.wikipedia.org/wiki/Value_add

http://en.wikipedia.org/wiki/Scalability

INDEX

A

align
    alignment xxii, 11, 58, 78, 79, 80, 81
assess 132, 151
    assessment xiv, 34, 36, 44, 119
audit 15, 28, 29, 78, 145, 177
authority
    authoritative, authorization xxii, 7, 12, 13, 19, 34, 60, 76, 89, 96, 102, 108, 109, 110, 111, 173, 176, 178

B

benchmark
    benchmarking xv, 77, 78
benefits
    benefit realization 155, 159
budget 133, 135, 140, 142, 147, 153
build-out xiii, xvii, xxiii, 3, 4, 31, 35, 36, 42, 47, 60, 61, 63, 89, 90, 91, 96, 97, 98, 100, 109, 110, 113, 137, 139, 146, 147, 173, 176, 177

C

case
    case study, case organization xi, 16, 60, 100, 113, 123, 125, 126, 128, 129, 151, 178, 184

Case Study 125
categorical
    categorical data 91, 92
champion 34, 143
change management 13, 29, 90, 102, 108, 109, 110, 111, 177, 178
CoE xiv, xxi, xxii, 12, 23, 116, 138, 139, 151, 156, 157
competitive 68, 119
Compliance 6, 12, 131, 142, 177
Continuous Data 94
customer xviii, 7, 64, 67, 88, 117, 134, 140, 147, 152, 158, 185

D

delivery
    deliverable xv, xxi, 4, 9, 10, 13, 14, 15, 16, 26, 30, 47, 63, 65, 66, 67, 68, 74, 80, 103, 106, 115, 116, 117, 119, 121, 122, 127, 128, 131, 132, 133, 137, 138, 139, 140, 142, 143, 144, 145, 146, 150, 151, 153, 154, 155, 156, 157, 158, 179, 180
demographic 91

E

employee 64, 150
Enterprise 130, 131, 144, 145, 154
EPM 139

execute 9, 65
Executive
    executive support, executive buy-in 158

F

factor 134, 135, 140, 148, 152, 153, 158, 159
finding 90, 109
framework 146
function 126, 128, 129, 131, 132, 133, 135, 137, 138, 139, 140, 143, 144, 145, 146, 150, 151, 152, 154, 156, 157, 159

G

gap
    gaps, gap analysis 144
Global 136, 154
goal 122, 144
governance 133, 134, 145, 146, 152, 153, 154, 156, 157, 158

H

human resources 64, 134, 140, 147, 152, 158

I

impact 126, 144, 145
implementation
    implement 151
improve
    improvement xv, xxi, 81, 116, 119, 120, 128, 132, 139, 140, 141, 142, 147, 154, 156

Insource 118
interaction
    interaction model 53, 60, 77

L

lesson
    lesson learned, lesson learning 12, 177
Lifecycle iii, xiii, 1, 3

M

maintain 15, 79, 120
methodology
    method 130, 132, 138, 146, 151

O

Office xiii, xiv, xxiii, 10, 122, 143, 154
outputs 53, 60
outsource 118, 119, 120, 123, 184

P

performance 141, 145, 147
PMO 125, 126, 127, 128, 129, 130, 132, 133, 134, 135, 137, 138, 139, 140, 143, 144, 145, 146, 147, 148, 150, 151, 152, 153, 154, 156, 157, 159
Portfolio 131, 133, 135, 136, 139, 146, 153, 154, 157, 159, 160
PPM 154, 157, 158, 159
process 139, 140, 144, 147, 152, 156, 158
Program 131, 133
Project 156, 157
project management 126, 128, 129, 132, 137, 138, 144, 145, 151

Project Manager
    program manager, project officer 131
project managers 154, 156, 158

Q

QRM
    Quality, Quality Risk Management xiv, 28, 29, 30, 32
qualitative 67, 148
quantitative 67, 148

R

RACI xiv
repository 6, 15, 51, 88
result 58, 59, 109, 135, 136, 140, 141, 142, 145, 153, 154, 158, 159
revitalize xiii, xvii
risk
    risk management, risk analysis xxii, 5, 14, 51, 64, 69, 71
roadmap xxiii, 3, 4, 5, 41, 44, 46, 79, 121, 147

S

scalability 20, 24, 25, 32
set-up xiii, xvii, xxiii, 3, 4, 31, 33, 34, 35, 36, 46, 47, 52, 56, 63, 89, 90, 91, 96, 97, 98, 100, 109, 110, 113, 137, 139, 144, 146, 147, 173, 176, 177
SME
    subject matter expert 35, 39, 120
sponsor
    sponsorship 76, 155
stakeholders 10, 128, 147

standard 130, 138, 143, 145, 147, 148, 152
standards
    RUP, COBIT, ITIL 156
    RUP, COBIT, ITIL, agile xv, xxii, 6, 11, 12, 14, 17, 30, 58, 60, 61, 76, 77, 81, 104, 105, 114, 116, 128, 132, 138, 145, 146, 147, 148, 151, 152, 153, 177, 179
survey
    web survey, survey results xi, xiii, xxiii, 32, 77, 90, 91, 92, 94, 96, 108, 109, 110, 111, 173, 181
sustainability xiii, xvii, xxiii, 3, 4, 31, 32, 37, 47, 63, 64, 76, 77, 78, 79, 83, 86, 88, 89, 90, 96, 97, 98, 100, 109, 110, 113, 117, 126, 145, 146, 147, 173, 176, 177, 178, 185
Sustainability 128, 134, 139, 146, 152, 157

T

templates 147
tool
    toolkit 18, 51, 58, 79, 91, 120

V

value 121, 155, 157
virtual
    virtualization 35, 94, 175
volume 142

APPENDIX A—INTERACTION MODEL

*Departments are listed based on organization's structure

*Department	Inputs to PMO	Collaboration with PMO	Outputs from PMO
Corporate Governance	This is a list of services and deliverables that this particular business functions provides the PMO with. (Corporate Governance is accountable to provide PMO)	This is a collaboration effort between the two business units.	This is a list of services and deliverables that the PMO would produces as a result of the input received from Corporate Governance (PMO is accountable to provide Corporate Governance) (PMO provides the PMO with.
Finance			
Marketing			
Sales			
IT			
Etc.			

APPENDIX B—ROADMAP

PMO Roadmap Outline (sample)

- Today – As is ?
  - Assessment of current status
  - Identify gaps and opportunities
  - Recommend future state

- Future - To be !
  - Review recommendation
  - Prioritize PMO functions and execution plan

- How to get there ?
  - Identify approach and timeframe
  - Identify resources and budget
  - Obtain sign-off and approval

APPENDIX C—WEB-BASED SURVEY LETTER

Dear Participant,

Today, Project Management Offices (PMOs) have been going through a transformation and changing how organizations view project management. PMOs have been taking on a more prominent role in their level of authority, structure, reporting line and mandate. It is because of the evolution of the PMO that I'm interested in you sharing your thoughts with me about the changes we have witnessed throughout the years.

My name is Waffa Karkukly and I am conducting a research project regarding the set-up and build-out and sustainability of PMOs. All answers will be anonymous and you will have a chance to proof read the results you provide. In addition, I will provide you with the overall results so you can compare and learn about similar and different success stories and challenges.

The survey is available at the following link:

http://app.fluidsurveys.com/surveys/waffa/pmo-setup/

The survey will take about 15 minutes and must be completed in one session. Upon survey completion, respondents will have the opportunity to provide their e-mail address to receive the overall research summary once it is completed. I wish to gather all survey responses prior to **May 20 2011.**

Thank you in advance for your help. If you would like more information, please contact me at **karkuklyw@yahoo.com**

Sincerely,
Waffa Karkukly, Ph.D
www.globalpmosolution.com

APPENDIX D—WEB SURVEY QUESTIONS

Section 1: PMOLC Questions

1- How many PMO's does your organization have (Please select only one)
   - Only one PMO
   - 2-3 PMO's
   - More than 3 PMO's

2- Where does your PMO reside (select all that applies)
   - Independent organization (outsourced or virtual PMO)
   - Corporate level
   - BU (Business Unit)
   - IT
   - Others (Please specify)

3- Where does your PMO report into? (Please select only one)
   - CEO
   - CFO
   - CIO
   - C level executive under CEO
   - Executive under C Level business side
   - Executive under C level IT side
   - Others (Please specify)

4- What level of management leads your PMO (select one)
   - C-Level
   - Executive (Someone who reports into a C-level)

- Director
- Manager
- Consultant
- Others (Please specify)

5- How do you define your PMO authority/influence in the company's hierarchy
   - PMO is involved at the highest boards C level discussion
   - PMO is involved through an executive who represent PMO at C level discussions
   - PMO is only involved at business unit level (departmental)
   - Others (Please specify)

6- What is your role in the PMO set-up and build
   - I built a none existing PMO
   - I re-built an existing PMO
   - I was hired to replace a previous PMO head
   - I was contracted to build the PMO only
   - Others (Please specify)

7- What is your role in the PMO sustainability and support
   - I support the PMO I built
   - I support an already built PMO
   - I was contracted to support a built PMO only
   - Others (Please specify)

8- Rank the complexity in the PMO lifecycle phases (set-up, build-out, sustainability) on scale from 1-5 1 lowest, 5 highest (1—least complex, 2—not as complex, 3—no difference, 4—complex, 5—most complex) Complexity = time/effort it takes to get the phase established
   - PMO setup (includes buy-in, funding, assessment, and proposed build)

- PMO build-out (includes setting of the PMO functions, standards, governance, etc)
- PMO sustainability (includes on-going support, continues improvement, training, etc)
- PMO change management regardless of a lifecycle phase
- PMO quality/ audit compliance regardless of a lifecycle phase

9- The skills of a PMO head to build a PMO may differ from those to run a PMO Select the role of the PMO lead in the PMO lifecycle phases (set-up, build-out, sustainability)
- PMO head skill set differ only between (set-up, build-out) vs. sustainability
- PMO head skill set differ only between set-up vs. (build-out, sustainability)
- PMO head skill set differ only between (set-up vs. build-out vs. sustainability
- PMO head skill set do not differ regardless of a phase
- PMO head skill set do differ regardless of a phase

10- What type of Authority does your PMO have, select only one
- Consulting /Services—Proposes, advise teams on how to run projects
- Knowledge Management—Manages, archive project details and lesson learn
- Compliance / Authoritative—Create and Set project management practices standards and monitor and control adherence of these standards

11- What are the unique challenges in the Setup and build-out phase (select all that app
- Funding
- Buy-in
- Leadership support

- Cost / Value
- Business case
- Skill set
- Governance
- Methodology adoption
- Others (Please specify)

12- What are the unique challenges in the sustainability phase
- Continuous improvement
- Reports / KPI
- Quality management / measurement
- Cost / Value
- Standards
- Project performance
- Project recovery
- Tools adoption
- Others (Please specify)

Section 2: PMO organizational questions

13- Do you believe change management and project management adoption in an organization is correlated to the level of PMO's authority
- The higher the authority, the more PMO's influence in change mgmt and PM adoption
- The lower the authority, the less PMO's influence in change mgmt and PM adoption
- The level of authority doesn't impact PMO's influence in change mgmt and PM adoption

14- In my organization, I can describe the level of executive buy-in as
- 100% Executive support—High
- 80% Executive support—Medium

- 50% Executive support—Low
- Less than 50% Executive support—very low

15- Does your PMO have responsibility for delivery of projects? (y/n)

16- How many Projects does your PMO manage in a year?
- 1-20 Projects
- 21-50 Projects
- 51-100 Projects
- More than 100 Projects

17- Please select one of the maturity levels below that best describes your PMO?
- Initial Level—ad hoc and chaotic; relies on the competence of individuals and no standards in place
- Repeatable Level—System and structure is in place based on previous experience.
- Defined Level—Standard system and structure organization wide of performed activities
- Managed Level—Established and measured processes against organizational goals; deviations are identified and managed.
- Optimizing Level—the entire organization is focused on continuous improvement

18- What functions does your PMO perform today (select all that applies)
- Portfolio management
- Methodology management
- Tools implementation
- Project/ program governance
- Project/ program standards
- Project manager training
- Resource capacity planning

- KPI and Reporting
- Project/ program assessment and quality check
- Others (Please specify)

19- What benefits does your Executive get today out of your PMO (Select all that applies)
- Improved Project Standardization
- Improved standardization of Operation
- Unified decision making across the Enterprise
- Faster access to quality information
- Better capacity planning (resource planning)
- Consistent project method of delivery
- Improved project governance and change control
- Improved project performance

20- What are the challenges that your PMO faces today? (select all that apply)
- Project management maturity,
- Portfolio management alignment
- Adoption of methodologies
- Adoption of tools,
- Leadership support,
- Lack of project managers kill set,
- Cost control,
- Others (Please specify)

21- In your organizations, project managers report into:
- PMO only
- Business Units only (IT included as a business unit)
- 50% PMO, 50% Business unit
- 20% PMO, 80% Business unit
- 80% PMO, 20% Business unit
- Other (Please specify)

Section 3: Demographic Questions

22- What is your geographic location? Select only one please
- US,
- Canada,
- Latin America
- Europe,
- Australia
- Asia Pacific
- Others (Please specify)

23- What is your Gender?
- Female
- Male

23- Enter your name and email if you wish to receive survey results

APPENDIX E—CASE STUDIES INTERVIEW QUESTIONNAIRE

The first group of questions focused on obtaining general information on their organizations, their practices, structure, and challenges

<u>General Questions</u>

1. Please provide brief background about your company in addition to the company public website
2. Provide brief background about yourself
3. Please provide background about your organization structure
4. Please provide a brief background about your PM practices
5. What was the main challenge the company is addressing in having a PMO?

The second group of questions inquires about whether they had project management practice before PMO, or PMO created the project practice. Whether PMO temporary or permanent, and whether the PMO insourced or outsourced, and whether the PPM practice is part of the PMO or not.

<u>Project Practices</u>

6. Please provide brief details pertaining to:
    a. Was project management practiced before having a PMO (y/n) how describe what was happening prior to having your PMO

b. If yes, how long after till a PMO existed in place and what motivated that
   c. If no, was creating a pmo to establish project practices and what other functions were expected of the established PMO
   d. Do you believe a project mgmt practice should exist before a PMO or the other way around and why?
7. Some believe that PMO is temporary, others believe it is permanent, please provide details:
   a. Is your PMO a permanent practice in the organization, or was it set as temporary for specific mgmt mandate?
   b. What was the driver of your decision/org decision to have it Temp or perm.
   c. What is the benefit of having it the way you have it, could you see it otherwise.
8. Please provide brief details pertaining to PMO insourcing or outsourcing:
   a. Is your PMO purely insourced, or outsourced, or hybrid.
   b. Whichever your answers maybe, please provide details to the functions insourced, outsourced, and are all project managers insourced or outsourced.
   c. Would you consider outsourcing why or why not
   d. If you would to outsource what tasks would you outsource
9. Please provide details pertaining to your PPM and PMO practice:
   a. Is your PPM practice separate from PMO (Y/N)
   b. If yes or no, in either case, please provide the driver to this decision and what were the benefits?
   c. In case PPM is not part of the PMO, how do you ensure the flow and handover between the two functions?
   d. Do both functions report into the same head/dept (what dept) or they report into separate heads/dept (what dept)

The third and last groups address the sustainability elements most notable value-add, and the impact on perceived Human resources value-add and customer value-add.

Sustainability Elements and value add

10. Do you consider your PMO function provides a value add (Y/N)
11. If yes, please quantify from the perspective of
    a. HR factor
    b. Quality factor
    c. Delivery factor
    d. Cost factor
12. How do you sustain performance?
13. Does your mandate change frequently and how do you describe your functions adaptability.
14. Would you be able to share some benefits quantitatively or qualitatively?

APPENDIX F—LIST OF ALL TABLES

PMO Set-up Steps	
New PMO	**Existing PMO**
Step 1: Identify the PMO sponsorship	**Step 1:** Assess current PMO sponsorship
Step 2: Identify PMO Type and Authority	**Step 2:** Assess effectiveness of current PMO Type and Authority
Step 3: Identify PMO Functions	**Step 3:** Assess current PMO Functions
Step 4: Identify PMO Staff	**Step 4:** Assess PMO Staff skill set
Step 5: Identify Project Managers Reporting Structure	**Step 5:** Assess current Project Managers Reporting Structure
Step 6: Identify PMO Interaction Model	**Step 6:** Assess effectiveness of current PMO interaction model
Step 7: Establish PMO Roadmap	**Step 7:** Re-establish PMO Roadmap

PMO Build-out Steps	
New PMO	**Existing PMO**
Step 1: Create PMO execution plan	**Step 1:** Create PMO execution plan
Step 2: Build Methodology	**Step 2:** Update Methodology
Step 3: Build Processes	**Step 3:** Update Processes
Step 4: Implement Tools	**Step 4:** Improve Tools effectiveness
Step 5: Build Other PMO functions	**Step 5:** Re-align Other PMO functions
Step 6: Build Interaction model	**Step 6:** Re-vitalize Interaction model
Step 7: Build Governance model	**Step 7:** Improve standard and governance model

PMO Sustainability Steps	
New PMO	**Existing PMO**
Step 1: Sustain reporting performance	**Step 1:** Re-align reporting performance
Step 2: Sustain support of PMO tools	**Step 2:** Re-align support of PMO tools
Step 3: Sustain training and mentoring programs	**Step 3:** Re-align training and mentoring programs
Step 4: Sustain PMO Staff skills and structure	**Step 4:** Re-align PMO Staff skills and structure
Step 5: Sustain executive commitments	**Step 5:** Re-align executive commitments
Step 6: Sustain continuous feedback loop	**Step 6:** Re-establish continuous feedback loop
Step 7: Sustain improvement action plan	**Step 7:** Re-establish improvement action plan

PMO Authority	PMO Type	PMO Functions
Consulting Services	Project or Program	Project Methodology
	Division PMO	Project Processes
		Project Reporting
	Enterprise PMO	Project Tools
		Project Manager Training
Knowledge Management	Project or Program	Project Methodology
	Division PMO	Project Processes
		Project Reporting
	Enterprise PMO	Project Repository
		Project Tools
Authoritative / Compliance	Project or Program	Project Methodology
	Division PMO	Project Processes
		Project Reporting
		Project Repository
	Enterprise PMO	Project Tools
	CoE PMO	Project Manager Development
		Project Delivery
	Global PMO	Project Portfolio

Author	PMO Type	Function / Role
Hill (2004)	PO	Applies effective practices for project performance and oversight, and employs standard life cycle processes when available
	Basic PMO	Introduces critical processes and practices of project management
	Standard PMO	Establishes and monitors use of a complete project management methodology
	Advanced PMO	Enhances content and monitors use of a comprehensive methodology
	Center Of Excellence (CoE)	Analyzes project management methodology and examines process variation in business units
Rad & Levin (2002)	Project or Program	A PMO supporting a single project or a group of related projects is recommended
	Division PMO	This PMO will establish standards and methodologies to follow in project management, will review and audit projects that are under way, and will provide mentoring support to project professionals.
	Enterprise PMO	This PMO is concerned with the enterprise of selection, prioritizing, and monitoring the value from project portfolio of an organization.
Crawford (2002)	Level 1- PCO	This is an office that typically handles large, complex single projects (such as Y2K project). It's specifically focused on one project, but that one project is so large and so complex that it requires multiple schedules, which may need to integrate into an overall program schedule.
	Level 2- Business Unit PO	The value of level 2 PO is that it begins to integrate resources at an organizational level. And it's at the organizational level that resource control begins to play a much higher value role in the payback of a project management system.
	Level 3 - Strategic PO	Only a corporate level organization can provide the coordination and broad perspective needed to select, prioritize, and monitor projects and programs that contribute to attainment of corporate strategy and this organization is the strategic project office.
Kendall & Rollins (2003)	Repository	The PMO serves as a source of information on projects, methodology and standards in this model. This model occurs most often in organizations that empower distributed, business-centric project ownership or with weak central governance
	Coach	The Coach Model is an extension of the Repository Model. It assumes a willingness to share some project management practices across functions and uses the PMO to coordinate the communication.
	Enterprise	This model usually implies a much larger investment and, therefore, usually has a stronger mission, charter and support than the previous two models. The most consolidated version of this organizational model concentrates senior project management expertise and execution within the PMO. Some or all project managers are staffed within the shared service model and consigned to projects as needed. The model assumes a governance process that involves the PMO in most projects, regardless of size.
	Deliver now	In this model, the emphasis is on delivering measurable value to the executive team within each 6-month period. At initial startup of this PMO, the resources focus on accelerated project deliveries across all major projects. This model has sponsorship at a very high executive level (CEO or Senior Vice President). Its metrics are tied directly to senior management performance

Scalability Model

PMO	Small	Medium	Large
Organization Resources	Less than 300	Between 300 - 1000	Over 1000
External Impact	Y/N	Y/N	Y/N
Internal Impact	Y/N	Y/N	Y/N
Business Process Change	H, M, L	H, M, L	H, M, L
Strategic Need	H, M, L	H, M, L	H, M, L
Geography	Local	National	Global
Reporting into	BU Lead	Executive	C-Level
Project Delivery Direct responsibility	Y/N	Y/N	Y/N
Number of Strategic projects	Less than 20	Between 20-100	Above 100
Number of Project Managers	Less than 10	Between 11-25	Above 25

PMO Authority	PMO Type	PMO Functions
Authoritative / Compliance	Project or Program	Project Methodology
	Division PMO	Project Processes
		Project Reporting
		Project Repository
	Enterprise PMO	Project Tools
	CoE PMO	Project Manager Development
		Project Delivery
	Global PMO	Project Portfolio

Project Manager Development Function

Function Inputs	Function Outputs
Skill set assessment tools to benchmark skills	Project managers skills benchmark
Organization goals	Career path and project culture
Current project management opportunities	Assignments based on skill set
Salary analysis compared to market standards	Competitive compensation relevant to skills